WIFT • SAMUEL TAYLOR COLERIDGE • EVELYN WAUGH • EZRA

SIMOV • CICERO • J. R. R. TOLKIEN • CARL SA_____L.

S PASSOS • MOLIERE • SUSAN SONTAG • N_____.

OMERSET MAUGHAM • VIRGINIA WOOLF • _____

ARA • NORMAN MAILER • JAMES JOYCE • GERTRUDE STEIN •

ORIS PASTERNAK • BERTOLT BRECHT • CHARLES DARWIN •

UDEN • EDNA ST. VINCENT MILLAY • ANTHONY BURGESS •

NGFELLOW • STEPHEN SPENDER • ELIZABETH BARRETT

ACKVILLE-WEST • STEPHANE MALLARME • PHILIP ROTH

NNESSEE WILLIAMS • ANDREW MARVELL • JOHN FOWLES • EMILE

CKETT • HENRY JAMES • CHARLOTTE BRONTË • HENRY FIELDING

DISON • JOSEPH HELLER • KARL MARX • SIGMUND FREUD •

LEXANDER POPE • HERMAN WOUK • IAN FLEMING • G. K.

LLOW • CHARLES KINGSLEY • FRANÇOISE SAGAN • JEAN-PAUL

TOPPARD • MARCEL PROUST • E. B. WHITE • IRIS MURDOCH •

BERT GRAVES • GEORGE BERNARD SHAW • ALDOUS HUXLEY •

EO TOLSTOY • D. H. LAWRENCE • WILLIAM GOLDING • H. G.

• TRUMAN CAPOTE • HAROLD PINTER • VIRGIL • OSCAR

EPHEN LONGSTREET • WILLA CATHER • JOHN CHEEVER •

The Booklover's Birthday Book

THE METROPOLITAN MUSEUM OF ART

THE NEW YORK PUBLIC LIBRARY

HARRY N. ABRAMS, INC., PUBLISHERS

NEW YORK

Special thanks are due to the entire staff of the Museum's Department of Prints and Photographs for their patience and cooperation throughout the research for this book. Valuable assistance was also obtained from the Museum's Drawings Department. The staff of The New York Public Library cooperated in every way; particular thanks go to Bobby Rainwater, curator of the Prints Department, and to Ruth Ann Stewart. All the illustrations in this book not otherwise marked are from the collections of The Metropolitan Museum of Art, photographed by the Museum's Photograph Studio.

COVER:
Fairy Tales (detail)
J. J. Shannon, American, 1862-1923
Oil on canvas
Arthur Hoppock Hearn Fund, 1913   13.143.1

Produced by the Department of Special Publications,
The Metropolitan Museum of Art
Composition by Finn Typographic Service, Inc.
Printing and binding by A. Mondadori, Verona, Italy
Designed by Peter Oldenburg
Sixth printing May 1990
ISBN 0-87099-377-1 The Metropolitan Museum of Art
ISBN 0-8109-0741-0 Abrams

Preface

"A good book," said the nineteenth-century novelist Martin Farquhar Tupper, "is the best of friends, the same to-day and for ever." Whether our taste runs to romance or mystery, to social history or verse, most of us have indeed found companionship in books, and have enjoyed discovering a writer's ideas, the fruits of the imagination, displayed in print.

Celebrated in these pages are the birthdays of over nine hundred writers. "Writers," here, are best defined as those who have made words work well for them. Hence, besides novelists, essayists, playwrights, and poets, the reader will find the names of historians, psychologists, and politicians. Lest the elusive February 29 slip past unmarked by a birthday, boundaries have been blurred a little to admit a composer, Gioacchino Rossini, who worked in unison with words.

Because the maximum number of names chosen for any one day was to be limited to three, selection forced out, on certain days, greater talent than it on other days allowed. July 26, for example, is the birthday of George Bernard Shaw, Carl Gustav Jung, Aldous Huxley, André Maurois, and Paul Gallico. All have earned a place in these pages; not all appear. Fame, literary merit, a wish to represent as broad as possible a range of talent have each influenced a slightly tyrannical selection process.

The fifteenth edition of the Encyclopædia Britannica was used to verify the spelling of many writers' names. A name might appear, however, in the form in which it is most commonly found in that writer's published work. No hard-and-fast rules have been applied. The same edition of the Encyclopædia Britannica was also used, whenever possible, to verify birthdays. The omission of certain writers, notably Tobias Smollett, Grace Metalious, and Aphra Behn, is due to the fact that no accurate record of their birthdays could be found. An exception was made for William Shakespeare (traditional birthday April 23) and for the indomitable Lady Mary Wortley Montagu, whose name appears on the day of her baptism, May 26. Spelling in the daily quotations follows that in the particular source used.

The 108 illustrations in this book, drawn from the collections of The New York Public Library and The Metropolitan Museum of Art, pay tribute to the centuries-old relationship between the writer and the artist. Research sometimes uncovered talents most aptly matched: William Hogarth, for instance, capturing the crucial moment of baptism of Laurence Sterne's *Tristram Shandy*; Hugh Thompson conveying Darcy's sneer in Jane Austen's *Pride and Prejudice;* Marc Chagall wrestling with Gogol's *Dead Souls.* Sometimes the combination of artist and writer was pleasingly unexpected: David Hockney for the Brothers Grimm, Aubrey Beardsley for Alexander Pope's "The Rape of the Lock," Jim Dine's picture of Dorian Gray. In the portraits of Thackeray, Henry Miller, and Günter Grass, writer and artist are one. The illustrations, which in no way represent a survey of book illustration, were subject to the same tyranny of selection described before.

For most of us there is something special about birthdays, particularly about shared birthdays. Born September 18? So was Samuel Johnson. One need not follow the stars to wonder a little about the possibility of transference of talent, or personality. If there is magic in this, it is harmless enough; may it work to good effect for those who use this book.

Barbara Anderman
Editor

The Booklover's Birthday Book

Woodcut by Hans Weiditz for
CICERO (January 3), *Officia M.T.C.* Augsburg, 1531

Gift of Felix M. Warburg, 1918   18.58.6

JANUARY 1

E. M. Forster 1879
J. D. Salinger 1919
Joe Orton 1933

_____

_____

_____

_____

How can I tell what I think till I see what I say.

E. M. Forster

JANUARY 2

Philip Freneau 1752
Robert Nathan 1894
Isaac Asimov 1920

_____

_____

_____

_____

It is possible that only human beings, of all living species, do not live entirely in the present.

Isaac Asimov

JANUARY 3

Cicero 106 B.C.
J. R. R. Tolkien 1892
Drieu La Rochelle 1893

_____

_____

_____

_____

Natural ability without education has more often raised a man to glory and virtue than education without natural ability.

Cicero

JANUARY 4

Jacob Grimm 1785
A. E. Coppard 1878

Cut off a person from all contact with tales and he will assuredly begin to invent some – probably about himself.

A. E. Coppard

Etching by David Hockney for
THE BROTHERS GRIMM (January 4, February 24), *Rapunzel*, from *Six Fairy Tales from the Brothers Grimm*
London: Petersburg Press, 1970

John B. Turner Fund, 1971   1971.515

JANUARY 5

Rudolf Eucken 1846
Friedrich Dürrenmatt 1921

The more human beings proceed by plan the more effectively they may hit by accident.

Friedrich Dürrenmatt

JANUARY 6

Carl Sandburg 1878
Wright Morris 1910
E. L. Doctorow 1931

_____

_____

_____

_____

Time is a great teacher.

Carl Sandburg

JANUARY 7

Louise Imogen Guiney 1861
Charles Péguy 1873
Gerald Durrell 1925

_____

_____

_____

_____

The triumph of demagogies is short-lived. But the ruins are eternal.

Charles Péguy

JANUARY 8

Wilkie Collins 1824
Charles Tomlinson 1927

_____

_____

_____

_____

It may be possible in novel-writing to present characters successfully without telling a story; but it is not possible to tell a story successfully without presenting characters.

Wilkie Collins

JANUARY 9

Henry B. Fuller 1857
Lascelles Abercrombie 1881
Simone de Beauvoir 1908

_____

_____

_____

_____

The word *love* has by no means the same sense for both sexes, and this is one cause of the serious misunderstandings that divide them.

Simone de Beauvoir

JANUARY 10

Aubrey de Vere 1814
Robinson Jeffers 1887

_____

_____

_____

_____

Prejudice, which sees what it pleases, cannot see what is plain.

Aubrey de Vere

JANUARY 11

William James 1842
Alan Paton 1903
Manfred B. Lee 1905

_____

_____

_____

_____

Be not afraid of life. Believe that life is worth living and your belief will help create the fact.

William James

JANUARY 12

Edmund Burke 1729
Jack London 1876
Ferenc Molnár 1878

_____

_____

_____

_____

It is a general popular error to imagine
the loudest complainers for the public
to be the most anxious for its welfare.

Edmund Burke

Wood engraving by Gustave Doré for
CHARLES PERRAULT (January 13), *Les contes de Perrault*
Paris: J. Hetzel & Cie, 1899

551   480 drawings to be done   *The Big Money*

Drawing by Reginald Marsh for
JOHN DOS PASSOS (January 14), *U.S.A.*, ca. 1946

Print Collection, The New York Public Library
Astor, Lenox and Tilden Foundations

Charles Perrault 1628
Prosper Jolyot de Crébillon 1674
Horatio Alger 1832

Angela Gauthier

Fear created gods; audacity created kings.

Prosper Jolyot de Crébillon

JANUARY 14

John Dos Passos 1896
Tillie Olsen 1913
Yukio Mishima 1925

_____

_____

_____

_____

Unused capacities atrophy, cease
to be.

Tillie Olsen

JANUARY 15

Molière 1622
Osip Mandelstam 1891

_____

_____

_____

_____

It infuriates me to be wrong when
I know I'm right.

Molière

Hand-colored steel engraving by
M. M. Geoffroy for MOLIERE (January 15),
Le bourgeois gentilhomme, from *Oeuvres
complètes de Molière*
Paris: Garnier Frères, 1850

Bequest of Alexandrine Sinsheimer, 1958   59.534.35

Vittorio Alfieri 1749
Laura Riding 1901
Susan Sontag 1933

To err is human, but the contrition felt
for the crime distinguishes the virtu-
ous from the wicked.

Vittorio Alfieri

"Open here I flung the shutter...."
Lithograph by Edouard Manet for
EDGAR ALLAN POE (January 19), *Le corbeau.* Paris: Richard Lesclide, 1875
Harris Brisbane Dick Fund, 1924   24.30.27(4)

Anne Brontë 1820
Nevil Shute 1899

Charles Louis de Secondat
Montesquieu 1689
A. A. Milne 1882
William Sansom 1912

Believe not those who say
   The upward path is smooth,
Lest thou shouldst stumble in the way
   And faint before the truth.

Anne Brontë

Cover design by Will Bradley for
RICHARD LE GALLIENNE (January 20), *The Romance of Zion Chapel*
New York: Frederick A. Stokes, 1898

Gift of Fern Bradley Dufner, 1972   1972.586.12

Success generally depends upon
knowing how long it takes to succeed.

Charles Louis de Secondat Montesquieu

JANUARY 19

Edgar Allan Poe 1809
Augustine Birrell 1850
Patricia Highsmith 1921

_____

_____

_____

_____

Sound loves to revel in a summer
night.

Edgar Allan Poe

JANUARY 20

Richard Le Gallienne 1866
Johannes V. Jensen 1873

_____

_____

_____

_____

Wild oats will get sown some time, and
one of the arts of life is to sow them at
the right time.

Richard Le Gallienne

JANUARY 21

R. P. Blackmur 1904

_____

_____

_____

_____

Myths . . . gossip grown old.

R. P. Blackmur

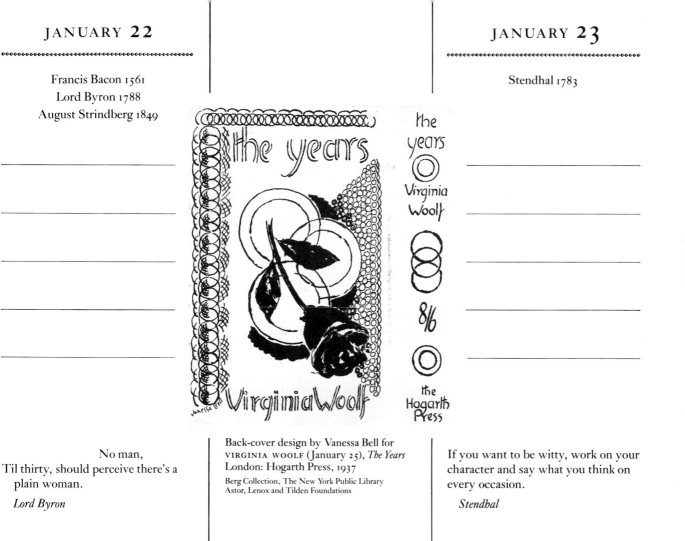

JANUARY 22

Francis Bacon 1561
Lord Byron 1788
August Strindberg 1849

_____

_____

_____

_____

_____

No man,
Til thirty, should perceive there's a
plain woman.

Lord Byron

Back-cover design by Vanessa Bell for
VIRGINIA WOOLF (January 25), *The Years*
London: Hogarth Press, 1937

Berg Collection, The New York Public Library
Astor, Lenox and Tilden Foundations

JANUARY 23

Stendhal 1783

_____

_____

_____

_____

_____

If you want to be witty, work on your
character and say what you think on
every occasion.

Stendhal

JANUARY 24

Pierre Beaumarchais 1732
Edith Wharton 1862
Vicki Baum 1888

_____

_____

_____

_____

Culture in France is an eminently
social quality, while in Anglo-Saxon
countries it might also be called
antisocial.

Edith Wharton

JANUARY 25

Robert Burns 1759
W. Somerset Maugham 1874
Virginia Woolf 1882

_____

_____

_____

_____

A bonny lass I will confess,
  Is pleasant to the e'e,
But without some better qualities
  She's no a lass for me.

Robert Burns

JANUARY 26

Eugène Sue 1804
M. M. Dodge 1830
Jules Feiffer 1929

_____

_____

_____

_____

Getting out of bed in the morning is an
act of false confidence.

Jules Feiffer

Friedrich Wilhelm von Schelling 1775
Lewis Carroll 1832

_____

_____

_____

_____

_____

Curtsy while you're thinking what to say. It saves time.

Lewis Carroll

Illustration by John Tenniel for
LEWIS CARROLL (January 27), *Alice's Adventures in Wonderland*
London and New York: Macmillan & Co., 1886

JANUARY 28

Sabine Baring-Gould 1834
Colette 1873

_____

_____

_____

_____

Give me a dozen such heartbreaks,
if that would help me to lose a couple
of pounds.

Colette

JANUARY 29

Thomas Paine 1737
Anton Chekhov 1860
Germaine Greer 1939

_____

_____

_____

_____

When we are planning for posterity,
we ought to remember that virtue
is not hereditary.

Thomas Paine

JANUARY 30

Walter Savage Landor 1775
Barbara Tuchman 1912
Shirley Hazzard 1931

Tyler Sample

_____

_____

_____

Every sect is a moral check on its
neighbor. Competition is as whole-
some in religion as in commerce.

Walter Savage Landor

JANUARY 31

John O'Hara 1905
Thomas Merton 1915
Norman Mailer 1923

Hot lead can be almost as effective coming from a linotype as from a firearm.

John O'Hara

Etching by Henri Matisse for
JAMES JOYCE (February 2), *Ulysses*. New York: Limited Editions Club, 1935
Rare Books and Manuscripts Division, The New York Public Library, Astor, Lenox and Tilden Foundations

GERTRUDE STEIN (February 3). Oil on canvas by Pablo Picasso, 1906
Bequest of Gertrude Stein, 1946   47.106

FEBRUARY I

Hugo von Hofmannsthal 1874
Langston Hughes 1902
S. J. Perelman 1904

What is culture? To know what
concerns one, and to know what it
concerns one to know.

Hugo von Hofmannsthal

FEBRUARY 2

Havelock Ellis 1859
James Joyce 1882
Ayn Rand 1905

_____

_____

_____

_____

_____

The artist, like the God of the creation, remains within or behind or beyond or above his handiwork, invisible, refined out of existence, indifferent, paring his fingernails.

James Joyce

FEBRUARY 3

Walter Bagehot 1826
Gertrude Stein 1874
James Michener 1907

_____

_____

_____

_____

_____

The greatest mistake is the trying to be more agreeable than you can be.

Walter Bagehot

FEBRUARY 4

Pierre Marivaux 1688
Jacques Prévert 1900
Betty Friedan 1921

_____

_____

_____

_____

_____

In this world, you must be a bit too kind in order to be kind enough.

Pierre Marivaux

FEBRUARY 5

Joris-Karl Huysmans 1848
Allan Seager 1906
William Burroughs 1914

_____

_____

_____

_____

A paranoid is a man who knows a little
of what's going on.

William Burroughs

FEBRUARY 6

Christopher Marlowe 1564
Ugo Foscolo 1778

Jeffrey LeDrew

_____

_____

_____

Nature, that fram'd us of four elements
Warring within our breasts for
   regiment,
Doth teach us all to have aspiring
   minds.

Christopher Marlowe

FEBRUARY 7

Samuel Butler 1612
Charles Dickens 1812
Sinclair Lewis 1885

_____

_____

_____

_____

An idea, like a ghost, according to
the common notion of ghosts, must
be spoken to a little before it will
explain itself.

Charles Dickens

FEBRUARY 8

John Ruskin 1819
Jules Verne 1828
Martin Buber 1878

_____

_____

_____

_____

_____

At least be sure that you go to the
author to get at *his* meaning, not to find
yours.

John Ruskin

Mr. Fezziwig's ball. Hand-colored etching by John Leech for
CHARLES DICKENS (February 7), *A Christmas Carol*. London: Chapman and Hall, 1843
The Arents Collections, The New York Public Library, Astor, Lenox and Tilden Foundations

Amy Lowell 1874
Brendan Behan 1923
Alice Walker 1944

Charles Lamb 1775
Boris Pasternak 1890
Bertolt Brecht 1898

Poetry and history are the textbooks
to the heart of man. . . .

Amy Lowell

Woodcut by Will Bradley for
CHARLES LAMB (February 10),
A Dissertation upon Roast Pig
Concord, Mass: The Sign of the Vine,
ca. 1903
Gift of Fern Bradley Dufner, The Will Bradley
Collection, 1952   52.625.45

Sentimentally I am disposed to harmony; but organically I am incapable
of a tune.

Charles Lamb

FEBRUARY II

Bernard Fontenelle 1657
Roy Fuller 1912
Sidney Sheldon 1917

_____

_____

_____

_____

_____

If I carried all the thoughts of the
world in my hand, I would take care
not to open it.

Bernard Fontenelle

"Enter these enchanted woods. . . ."
Photogravure by William Hyde for
GEORGE MEREDITH (February 12), *The Nature Poems*
London: Constable & Co., 1907

The Elisha Whittelsey Collection,
The Elisha Whittelsey Fund, 1969   69.589.1

FEBRUARY 12

Thomas Campion 1567
Charles Darwin 1809
George Meredith 1828

_____

_____

_____

_____

There is no freedom for the weak.
George Meredith

Color lithograph by Auguste Rodin for
OCTAVE MIRBEAU (February 16), *Le jardin des supplices*. Paris: Ambroise Vollard, 1902
Harris Brisbane Dick Fund, 1923   23.19.1

FEBRUARY 13

Eleanor Farjeon 1881
Ricardo Güiraldes 1886
Georges Simenon 1903

_____

_____

_____

_____

I write fast, because I have not the
brains to write slow.

Georges Simenon

FEBRUARY 14

Israel Zangwill 1864
George Jean Nathan 1882

_____

_____

_____

_____

Fortunately, religion depends as
little upon theology as love upon
phrenology.

Israel Zangwill

FEBRUARY 15

Jeremy Bentham 1748
Alfred North Whitehead 1861
Sax Rohmer 1886

_____

_____

_____

_____

Tyranny and anarchy are never far
asunder.

Jeremy Bentham

Henry Adams 1838
Octave Mirbeau 1850
Van Wyck Brooks 1886

_____

_____

_____

_____

Young men have a passion for regarding their elders as senile.

Henry Adams

Dorothy Canfield Fisher 1879
Bess Streeter Aldrich 1881
Chaim Potok 1929

_____

_____

_____

_____

One of the many things nobody ever tells you about middle age is that it's such a nice change from being young.

Dorothy Canfield Fisher

Sholem Aleichem 1859
André Breton 1896
Toni Morrison 1931

_____

_____

_____

_____

. . . writing an autobiography and making a spiritual will are practically the same.

Sholem Aleichem

FEBRUARY 19

David Garrick 1717
Kay Boyle 1903
Carson McCullers 1917

_____

_____

_____

_____

FEBRUARY 20

Hesketh Pearson 1887
Georges Bernanos 1888
Russel Crouse 1893

James Cocchio

_____

_____

_____

L'AN SUAVE

par
André BRETON

Fun gives you a forcible hug, and
shakes laughter out of you, whether
you will or no.

David Garrick

Etching by Marie Laurencin for
ANDRÉ BRETON (February 18),
"L'an suave," from *Evantail*
Paris: Editions de la Nouvelle Revue
Française, 1922
Harris Brisbane Dick Fund, 1923   23.19.3

2.

. . . the most dangerous shortsighted-
ness consists in underestimating the
mediocre. . . .

Georges Bernanos

John Henry Newman 1801
W. H. Auden 1907
Erma Bombeck 1927

_____

_____

_____

_____

Fatalism is the refuge of a conscience-
stricken mind, maddened at the sight
of evils which it has brought upon
itself, and cannot remove.

John Henry Newman

Illustration by Winslow Homer for
JAMES RUSSELL LOWELL (February 22),
The Courtin'
Boston: J. R. Osgood & Co., 1874
Gift of Sinclair Hamilton, 1941   41.112

James Russell Lowell 1819
Edna St. Vincent Millay 1892
Sean O'Faolain 1900

_____

_____

_____

_____

In general those who nothing have
to say
Contrive to spend the longest time
in doing it.

James Russell Lowell

FEBRUARY **23**

Samuel Pepys 1633
W. E. B. Du Bois 1868
Karl Jaspers 1883

Strange to see how a good dinner and feasting reconciles everybody.

Samuel Pepys

GEORGE MOORE (February 24)
Oil on canvas by Edouard Manet, ca. 1879
Gift of Mrs. Ralph J. Hines, 1955   55.193

FEBRUARY **24**

❖❖❖❖❖❖❖❖❖❖❖❖❖❖❖❖❖❖❖❖❖❖❖❖❖❖❖❖❖❖❖❖❖❖

Pico della Mirandola 1463
Wilhelm Grimm 1786
George Moore 1852

_____

_____

_____

_____

An insufficient talent is the cruelest of
all temptations.

George Moore

VICTOR HUGO (February 26). Etching with drypoint by Auguste Rodin, 1886
Rogers Fund, 1916   16.37.1

FEBRUARY 25

Carlo Goldoni 1707
Benedetto Croce 1866
Anthony Burgess 1917

_____

_____

_____

_____

_____

America, on one level, is a great old-movie museum.

Anthony Burgess

FEBRUARY 26

Victor Hugo 1802

_____

_____

_____

_____

The malicious have a dark happiness.

Victor Hugo

FEBRUARY 27

Henry Wadsworth Longfellow 1807
John Steinbeck 1902
Lawrence Durrell 1912

_____

_____

_____

_____

Most people would succeed in small things if they were not troubled by great ambitions.

Henry Wadsworth Longfellow

FEBRUARY 28

Michel de Montaigne 1533
Stephen Spender 1909

_____

_____

_____

_____

_____

No man is exempt from saying silly
things; the mischief is to say them
deliberately.

Michel de Montaigne

FEBRUARY 29

Gioacchino Rossini 1792

_____

_____

_____

_____

_____

There is no worse robber than a bad
book.

Italian proverb

MARCH 1

William Dean Howells 1837
Lytton Strachey 1880
Robert Lowell 1917

_____

_____

_____

_____

_____

Perhaps of all the creations of man
language is the most astonishing.

Lytton Strachey

MARCH 2

Camille Desmoulins 1760
Tom Wolfe 1931
John Irving 1942

_____

_____

_____

_____

The true patriot doesn't know people,
he only knows principles.

Camille Desmoulins

"That sweet young blonde,
who arrives by most trains."
Illustration by Augustus
Hoppin for WILLIAM DEAN HOWELLS
(March 1), *Suburban Sketches*
Boston: J. R. Osgood and Co., 1875
Gift of Bella C. Landauer, 1949   49.130.6

MARCH 3

Edmund Waller 1606
Thomas Otway 1652
William Godwin 1756

_____

_____

_____

_____

Poets lose half the praise they should
     have got,
Could it be known what they
     discreetly blot.

Edmund Waller

Charles Dibdin 1745
Johann Wyss 1782
Alan Sillitoe 1928

Did you ever hear of Captain Wattle?
He was all for love, and a little for the
bottle.

Charles Dibdin

Illustration by Diego Rivera for
STUART CHASE (March 8), *Mexico: A Study of Two Americas*. New York: Macmillan Co., 1934
The Elisha Whittelsey Collection, The Elisha Whittelsey Fund, 1969   69.589.8

MARCH 5

Constance Fenimore Woolson 1840
Frank Norris 1870
Christopher Hibbert 1924

_____

_____

_____

_____

There are more things in San Francisco's Chinatown than are dreamed of in Heaven and earth.

Frank Norris

MARCH 6

Elizabeth Barrett Browning 1806
Ring Lardner 1885
Gabriel García Márquez 1928

_____

_____

_____

_____

The child's sob in the silence curses deeper
Than the strong man in his wrath.

Elizabeth Barrett Browning

MARCH 7

Alessandro Manzoni 1785
Kobo Abé 1924

_____

_____

_____

_____

You must always explain things frankly and explicitly to your lawyer. . . it is for him to embroil them afterwards.

Alessandro Manzoni

Kenneth Grahame 1859
Stuart Chase 1888
Eric Linklater 1899

_____

_____

_____

_____

_____

Illustration by Maxfield Parrish for
KENNETH GRAHAME (March 8),
The Golden Age
London and New York: John Lane, 1900
Gift of Miss Fairchild Bowler, 1965   65.518.2

Grown-up people really ought to be
more careful. Among themselves it
may seem but a small thing to give
their word and take back their word.

Kenneth Grahame

David Garnett 1892
Vita Sackville-West 1892
Mickey Spillane 1918

Blair Sorenson
_____

_____

_____

_____

_____

It is never wise to disregard the sagac-
ity of those who do not learn their lore
from books.

Vita Sackville-West

MARCH 10

Friedrich von Schlegel 1772
Pedro Antonio de Alarcón 1833
Jacob Wasserman 1873

_____

_____

_____

_____

A historian is a prophet in reverse.

Friedrich von Schlegel

•••••••••••

Drawing by C. N. Cochin for
TORQUATO TASSO (March 11),
La gerusalemme liberata, 1784–88

MARCH 11

Torquato Tasso 1544
Madame d'Epinay 1726
D. J. Enright 1920

Jay Sanders

_____

_____

_____

Honor, glory, praise, renown, and
fame– each is but an echo, a shade,
a dream, a flower that is blasted
with every wind and spoiled with
every shower.

Torquato Tasso

MARCH 12

George Berkeley 1685
Gabriele D'Annunzio 1863
Edward Albee 1928

_____

_____

_____

_____

He who says there is no such thing
as an honest man, you may be sure
is himself a knave.

George Berkeley

MARCH 13

Percival Lowell 1855
Hugh Walpole 1884

_____

_____

_____

_____

'Tisn't life that matters! 'Tis the courage you bring to it.

Hugh Walpole

Albert Einstein 1879
John Wain 1925

Lady Gregory 1852
Lionel Johnson 1867
Richard Ellmann 1918

STEPHANE MALLARME (March 18)
Etching by Paul Gauguin, 1891
Harris Brisbane Dick Fund, 1936   36.11.10

Make everything as simple as possible,
but not simpler.

Albert Einstein

I know you: solitary griefs,
Desolate passions, aching hours!

Lionel Johnson

MARCH 16

Ernest Feydeau 1821
Sully Prudhomme 1839

The slaying of Achilles.
Woodcut for OVID (March 20), *Metamorphoses*
Venice: Luc'Antonio Giunta, 1501
Rogers Fund, 1922   22.16

Habit is an outsider that supplants reason in us.

Sully Prudhomme

MARCH 17

Moncure Daniel Conway 1832
Paul Green 1894

_____

_____

_____

_____

Tomorrow's another day.

Paul Green

MARCH 18

Stéphane Mallarmé 1842
Wilfred Owen 1893
John Updike 1932

_____

_____

_____

_____

Dreams have as much influence as actions.

Stéphane Mallarmé

MARCH 19

Richard F. Burton 1821
Irving Wallace 1916
Philip Roth 1933

_____

_____

_____

_____

Do what thy manhood bids thee do,
 from none but self expect applause;
He noblest lives and noblest dies who
 makes and keeps his self-made laws.

Richard F. Burton

MARCH 20

Ovid 43 B.C.
Friedrich Hölderlin 1770
Henrik Ibsen 1828

_____

_____

_____

_____

A community is like a ship; everyone
ought to be prepared to take the helm.

Henrik Ibsen

MARCH 21

Jean Paul Friedrich Richter 1763
Phyllis McGinley 1905

_____

_____

_____

_____

There is nothing more beautiful than
cheerfulness in an old face.

Jean Paul Friedrich Richter

MARCH 22

John Banister Tabb 1845
Nicholas Monsarrat 1910

_____

_____

_____

_____

How many an acorn falls to die
For one that makes a tree!
How many a heart must pass me by
For one that cleaves to me!

John Banister Tabb

MARCH 23

Paul Leicester Ford 1865
Roger Martin du Gard 1881
Erich Fromm 1900

_____

_____

_____

_____

If one doesn't do good by natural in-
clination let it be out of desperation;
or at least so as not to do evil.

Roger Martin du Gard

Illustration by George Barbier for
PAUL VERLAINE (March 30), *Fêtes galantes*
Paris: H. Piazza, 1928
Lent by Mr. and Mrs. Bryan Holme

William Morris 1834
Olive Schreiner 1855
Lawrence Ferlinghetti 1919

If you want a golden rule that will fit everybody, this is it: Have nothing in your houses that you do not know to be useful, or believe to be beautiful.

William Morris

Etching by Marc Chagall for
NIKOLAI GOGOL (March 31), *Les âmes mortes*. Paris: Tériade, 1948

MARCH 25

Antonio Fogazzaro 1842
Mary Webb 1881
Flannery O'Connor 1925

Saddle your dreams afore you ride 'em.

Mary Webb

MARCH 26

A. E. Housman 1859
Robert Frost 1874
Tennessee Williams 1914

The best way out is always through.

Robert Frost

MARCH 27

Alfred de Vigny 1797
Shusaku Endo 1923

What is a great life but a youthful intention carried out in maturity?

Alfred de Vigny

MARCH 28

Maxim Gorky 1868
Nelson Algren 1909
Mario Vargas Llosa 1936

_____

_____

_____

_____

It is always disagreeable when a person we consider our inferior likes or loathes the same things we do, thereby becoming our equal.

Maxim Gorky

MARCH 29

Howard Lindsay 1889

_____

_____

_____

_____

Clever liars give details, but the cleverest don't.

Anonymous

MARCH 30

Moses Maimonides 1135
Paul Verlaine 1844
Sean O'Casey 1880

_____

_____

_____

_____

Anticipate charity by preventing poverty. . . .

Moses Maimonides

Andrew Marvell 1621
Nikolai Gogol 1809
John Fowles 1926

Abbé Prévost 1697
Anthelme Brillat-Savarin 1755
Milan Kundera 1929

EMILE ZOLA (April 2)
Crayon drawing by F. Graetz, n.d.
Print Collection, The New York Public Library
Astor, Lenox and Tilden Foundations

But at my back I always hear
Time's wingèd chariot hurrying near;
And yonder all before us lie
Deserts of vast eternity.

Andrew Marvell

You first parents of the human
race . . . who ruined yourself for an
apple, what might you not have done
for a truffled turkey?

Anthelme Brillat-Savarin

APRIL 2

Hans Christian Andersen 1805
Emile Zola 1840

_____

_____

_____

_____

Perfection is such a nuisance that
I often regret having cured myself
of using tobacco.

Emile Zola

Rip Van Winkle. Etching by
F. O. C. Darley for WASHINGTON IRVING
(April 3), *Sketchbook of Geoffrey Crayon Gent.*
New York: G. P. Putnam, Hurd &
Houghton, 1865

Print Collection, The New York Public Library
Astor, Lenox and Tilden Foundations

APRIL 3

George Herbert 1593
Washington Irving 1783
Edward Everett Hale 1822

_____

_____

_____

_____

Whenever a man's friends begin to
compliment him about looking young,
he may be sure that they think he is
growing old.

Washington Irving

APRIL 4

Robert Emmet Sherwood 1896
Tristan Tzara 1896
Maya Angelou 1928

_____

_____

_____

_____

The duty of dramatists is to express
their times and guide the public
through the perplexities of those
times.

Robert Emmet Sherwood

APRIL 5

Thomas Hobbes 1588
Giacomo Casanova 1725
Algernon Swinburne 1837

_____

_____

_____

_____

If you want to make people weep, you
must weep yourself. If you want to
make people laugh, your face must
remain serious.

Giacomo Casanova

APRIL 6

Jean-Baptiste Rousseau 1671
Lincoln Steffens 1866
John Betjeman 1906

_____

_____

_____

_____

. . . men do not seek the truth. It is
truth that pursues men who run away
and will not look around.

Lincoln Steffens

Color lithograph by Joan Mirò for
TRISTAN TZARA (April 4), *Parler seul, poème*. Paris: Maeght, 1948
Spencer Collection, The New York Public Library, Astor, Lenox and Tilden Foundations

William Wordsworth 1770
Gabriele Mistral 1889
Donald Barthelme 1931

The wiser mind
Mourns less for what age takes away
Than what it leaves behind.

William Wordsworth

APRIL 8

Margaret Ayer Barnes 1886
C. M. Bowra 1898

_____

_____

_____

_____

The artist who really creates something creates it for ever, but the scholar is at the mercy of expanding knowledge and changing habits of thought.

C. M. Bowra

APRIL 9

Charles Baudelaire 1821

Kevin Mones

_____

_____

_____

_____

It is by universal misunderstanding that all agree. For if, by ill luck, people understood each other, they would never agree.

Charles Baudelaire

"Apparelled in celestial light."
Wood engraving by G. L. Gowee
after Childe Hassam for
WILLIAM WORDSWORTH (April 7),
Ode. Intimations of Immortality
Boston: D. Lothrop and Co., 1884

Anonymous Gift, 1940   40.131.1

APRIL 10

William Hazlitt 1778
Clare Boothe Luce 1903
Paul Theroux 1941

_____

_____

_____

_____

As we advance in life, we acquire a
keener sense of the value of time.
Nothing else, indeed, seems of any
consequence; and we become misers
in this respect.

William Hazlitt

APRIL 11

Christopher Smart 1722
Glenway Wescott 1901
Mark Strand 1934

_____

_____

_____

_____

As you from all and each expect,
For all and each thy love direct,
　And render as you reap.

Christopher Smart

APRIL 12

Aleksandr Ostrovsky 1823

_____

_____

_____

_____

It's all papers and forms, the entire
Civil Service is like a fortress made of
papers, forms, and red tape.

Aleksandr Ostrovsky

APRIL 13

Samuel Beckett 1906
Eudora Welty 1909
John Braine 1922

Being a writer in a library is rather like being a eunuch in a harem.

John Braine

CHARLES BAUDELAIRE (April 9)
Etching by Edouard Manet, 1862
Print Collection, The New York Public Library
Astor, Lenox and Tilden Foundations

APRIL 14

James Branch Cabell 1879
Arnold Toynbee 1889

The optimist proclaims that we live in the best of all possible worlds; and the pessimist fears this is true.

James Branch Cabell

Henry James 1843

Anatole France 1844
John Millington Synge 1871
Kingsley Amis 1922

Illustration by Maurice Boutet de Monvel
for ANATOLE FRANCE (April 16), *Filles
et garçons*
Paris: Hachette et Cie, n.d.
Harris Brisbane Dick Fund, 1924   24.46.20

It's a complex fate, being an American,
and one of the responsibilities it entails
is fighting against a superstitious
valuation of Europe.

Henry James

One must learn to think well before
learning to think; afterward it proves
too difficult.

Anatole France

Henry Vaughan 1622
Isak Dinesen 1885
Thornton Wilder 1897

Richard Harding Davis 1864
Stephen Longstreet 1907

Everybody's always talking about people breaking into houses . . . but there are more people in the world who want to break out of houses.

Thornton Wilder

Engraving by Etienne Fessard after Hubert François Gravelot for
HENRY FIELDING (April 22),
Histoire de Tom Jones ou l'enfant trouvé
London: Jean Nourse, 1750
Harris Brisbane Dick Fund, 1927   27.79

No civilized person ever goes to bed the same day he gets up.

Richard Harding Davis

APRIL 19

José Echegaray 1832
Richard Hughes 1900

Matthew Garrett

_____

_____

_____

_____

. . . I have been taught that gossip,
whether inspired by malice or
not . . . begins in a lie and generally
ends in truth.

José Echegaray

APRIL 20

Herman Bang 1857

_____

_____

_____

_____

_____

Better ask twice than lose your way
once.

Danish proverb

APRIL 21

Charlotte Brontë 1816

_____

_____

_____

_____

_____

. . . as much good-will may be con-
veyed in one hearty word as in many.

Charlotte Brontë

rawing by Johann Heinrich Füssli for
ILLIAM SHAKESPEARE (April 23 trad.), *The Merry Wives of Windsor*, 1790
quest of Harry G. Sperling, 1971

Henry Fielding 1707
Immanuel Kant 1724
Ellen Glasgow 1874

_____

_____

_____

_____

_____

To invent good stories, and to tell them
well, are possibly very rare talents,
and yet I have observed few persons
who have scrupled to aim at both. . . .

    Henry Fielding

William Shakespeare 1564 (trad.)
Ngaio Marsh 1899
Vladimir Nabokov 1899

_____

_____

_____

_____

Fortune brings in some boats that are not steer'd.

William Shakespeare

Anthony Trollope 1815
Robert Penn Warren 1905

_____

_____

_____

_____

Wars about trifles . . . are always bitter, especially among neighbours. When the differences are great, and the parties comparative strangers, men quarrel with courtesy.

Anthony Trollope

Walter de la Mare 1873

_____

_____

_____

_____

. . . romance is invariably flavoured with the extreme.

Walter de la Mare

Marcus Aurelius 121
Alice Cary 1820
Bernard Malamud 1914

_____

_____

_____

_____

Herbert Spencer 1820
C. Day Lewis 1904

_____

_____

_____

_____

Mr. Alacadacca. Illustration by
Claude Lovat Fraser for
WALTER DE LA MARE (April 25),
Peacock Pie. A Book of Rhymes
London: Constable & Co., 1924
Gift of Miss Fairchild Bowler, 1965   65.620.1

Discontent brings neither cold cash
nor true love. . . .

Bernard Malamud

The ultimate result of shielding men
from the effects of folly is to fill the
world with fools.

Herbert Spencer

Harper Lee 1926
Diane Johnson 1934

In Monroeville, well, they're Southern people, and if they know you are working at home they think nothing of walking right in for coffee. But they wouldn't dream of interrupting you on the golf course.

Harper Lee

Edward Rowland Sill 1841
Rod McKuen 1938

At the punch-bowl's brink
Let the thirsty think
　　What they say in Japan:
"First the man takes a drink,
Then the drink takes a drink,
　　Then the drink takes the man!"

Edward Rowland Sill

Sir John Lubbock 1834
John Crowe Ransom 1888
Annie Dillard 1945

The important thing is not so much that every child should be taught, as that every child should be given the wish to learn.

Sir John Lubbock

MAY **1**

Joseph Addison 1672
Pierre Teilhard de Chardin 1881
Joseph Heller 1923

We are always doing something
for Posterity, but I would fain see
Posterity do something for us.

Joseph Addison

Wood engraving by Edmund Evans after a design by Kate Greenaway for
ROBERT BROWNING (May 7), *The Pied Piper of Hamelin*. London: George Routledge
and Sons, n.d.

Gift of Fred Baum, 1963   63.686

John Galt 1779
Jerome K. Jerome 1859

Niccolò Machiavelli 1469
May Sarton 1912
William Inge 1913

Illustration by M. B. Prendergast for
J. M. BARRIE (May 9), *My Lady Nicotine*
Boston: Joseph Knight Co., 1896
Gift of Steuben Glass, 1952   52.539.2

It is impossible to enjoy idling
thoroughly unless one has plenty of
work to do.

Jerome K. Jerome

Men are more ready to offend one who
desires to be beloved than one who
wishes to be feared.

Niccolò Machiavelli

MAY 4

William H. Prescott 1796
Thomas Kinsella 1928

Kari Heninger Murdock

The surest test of the civilization of a people– at least as sure as any– afforded by mechanical art is to be found in their architecture.

William H. Prescott

MAY 5

Sören Kierkegaard 1813
Karl Marx 1818
Henryk Sienkiewicz 1846

Life can only be understood back-wards; but it must be lived forwards.

Sören Kierkegaard

MAY 6

Sigmund Freud 1856
Randall Jarrell 1914
Theodore H. White 1915

Michael Kendrick

Two can live as cheaply as one– if they both have good jobs.

Sigmund Freud

MAY 7

Robert Browning 1812
Rabindranath Tagore 1861
Archibald MacLeish 1892

_____

_____

_____

_____

Grow old along with me!
The best is yet to be,
The last of life, for which the first
    was made.
Our times are in his hand.

Robert Browning

MAY 8

Edward Gibbon 1737
Edmund Wilson 1895
Thomas Pynchon 1937

_____

_____

_____

_____

There's only one thing worse than the
man who will argue over anything,
and that's the man who will argue over
nothing.

Edward Gibbon

MAY 9

J. M. Barrie 1860
José Ortega y Gasset 1883
Richard Adams 1920

_____

_____

_____

_____

I am not young enough to know everything.

J. M. Barrie

MAY 10

Benito Pérez Galdós 1843
Eric Berne 1910

We're born princes and the civilizing
process turns us into frogs.

Eric Berne

There was an Old Man of Columbia, who was thirsty, and called out for some beer;
But they brought it quite hot, in a small copper pot,
Which disgusted that man of Columbia.

There was an Old Man in a tree, who was horribly bored by a Bee;
When they said, "Does it buzz?" he replied, "Yes, it does!
It's a regular brute of a Bee!"

Illustration by EDWARD LEAR (May 12) for
A Book of Nonsense. London: Frederick Warne and Co., ca. 1870

Gift of Mr. and Mrs. Bryan Holme, 1980

Color lithograph by Raoul Dufy for
ALPHONSE DAUDET (May 13), *Adventures prodigeuses de Tartarin de Tarascon*
Paris: Scripta et Picta, 1937

Spencer Collection, The New York Public Library
Astor, Lenox and Tilden Foundations

Thomas Noel 1799
Camilo José Cela 1916

_____

_____

_____

_____

_____

By the waters of Life we sat together,
  Hand in hand, in the golden days
Of the beautiful early summer
    weather,
  When skies were purple and breath
    was praise.

Thomas Noel

MAY 12

Edward Lear 1812
Dante Gabriel Rossetti 1828
Philip Wylie 1902

_____

_____

_____

_____

Material blessings, when they pass
beyond the category of need, are
weirdly fruitful of headache.

Philip Wylie

MAY 13

Alphonse Daudet 1840
Daphne du Maurier 1907

_____

_____

_____

_____

He who has a reputation for early
rising can sleep till noon.

Alphonse Daudet

MAY 14

Dante Alighieri 1265
Hall Caine 1853

_____

_____

_____

_____

He who sees a need and waits to be
asked for help is as unkind as if he had
refused it.

Dante Alighieri

MAY 15

L. Frank Baum 1856
Edwin Muir 1887
Katherine Anne Porter 1890

_____

_____

_____

_____

The mind and heart sometimes get
another chance, but if anything hap-
pens to the poor old human frame,
why, it's just out of luck, that's all.

Katherine Anne Porter

MAY 16

Friedrich Rückert 1788
Douglas Southall Freeman 1886

_____

_____

_____

_____

The coward, the self-seeker, the
glutton, the sentimentalist– these
are not eliminated by war. They are
aggravated.

Douglas Southall Freeman

MAY 17

Robert Surtees 1803
Henri Barbusse 1873
Dorothy Richardson 1873

_____

_____

_____

_____

They invent a legend to put the blame
for the existence of humanity on
women and, if she wants to stop it,
they talk about the wonders of civilization and the sacred responsibilities of
motherhood. They can't have it both
ways.

Dorothy Richardson

Christopher North 1785
Bertrand Russell 1872

The time you enjoy wasting is not wasted time.

Bertrand Russell

Dante and Beatrice with the blessed souls.
Engraving for DANTE ALIGHIERI (May 14), *La divina commedia*
Venice: Appresso Giovambattista Marchiō Sessa et Fratelli, 1578

Gift of Francis Leonard Cater, 1958   58.584

MAY 19

Johann Fichte 1762

Pen and India ink drawing by
William Wallace Denslow for
L. FRANK BAUM (May 15),
The Wonderful Wizard of Oz, 1900
Print Collection, The New York Public Library
Astor, Lenox and Tilden Foundations

A man can do what is his duty; and
when he says "I cannot," he means,
"I will not."

Johann Fichte

MAY 20

Honoré de Balzac 1799
Sigrid Undset 1882
Margery Allingham 1904

Solitude is fine but you need someone
to tell you that solitude is fine.

Honoré de Balzac

Alexander Pope 1688
Robert Creeley 1926

Gérard du Nerval 1808
Arthur Conan Doyle 1859
Vance Packard 1914

Wood engraving by Charles Conder for
HONORE DE BALZAC (May 20),
La fille aux yeux d'or
London: Leonard Smithers, 1896
The Elisha Whittelsey Collection,
The Elisha Whittelsey Fund, 1967   67.807.6

A man should never be ashamed to
own he has been in the wrong, which is
but saying, in other words, that he is
wiser today than he was yesterday.

Alexander Pope

When you have eliminated the impossible, whatever remains, however
improbable must be the truth.

Arthur Conan Doyle

Thomas Hood 1799
Margaret Fuller 1810
Pär Lagerkvist 1891

Two persons love in one another
the future good which they aid one
another to unfold.

  Margaret Fuller

Illustration by Aubrey Beardsley for
ALEXANDER POPE (May 21),
The Rape of the Lock
London: Leonard Smithers, 1896

The Elisha Whittelsey Collection,
The Elisha Whittelsey Fund, 1967   67.807.7

MAY 24

R. B. Cunninghame Graham 1852
Mikhail Sholokhov 1905
Arnold Wesker 1932

_____

_____

_____

_____

. . . anyone who has been cajoled, trapped or persuaded into any kind of promise, usually looks upon himself more as a victim than as a criminal, when he succumbs to fate.

R. B. Cunninghame Graham

MAY 25

Edward Bulwer-Lytton 1803
Ralph Waldo Emerson 1803
Theodore Roethke 1908

_____

_____

_____

_____

Tomorrow a stranger will say with masterly good sense precisely what we have thought and felt all the time, and we shall be forced to take with shame our own opinion from another.

Ralph Waldo Emerson

MAY 26

Lady Mary Wortley Montagu 1689
Edmond de Goncourt 1822

_____

_____

_____

_____

I give myself sometimes admirable advice, but I am incapable of taking it.

Lady Mary Wortley Montagu

MAY 27

Louis-Ferdinand Céline 1894
John Cheever 1912
Herman Wouk 1915

If you aren't rich, you should always look useful.

Louis-Ferdinand Céline

MAY 28

Thomas Moore 1779
Ian Fleming 1908
Walker Percy 1916

So Life's year begins and closes;
  Days though shortening still can shine;
What though youth gave love and roses,
  Age still leaves us friends and wine.

Thomas Moore

MAY 29

G. K. Chesterton 1874

I do not see ghosts; I only see their inherent probability.

G. K. Chesterton

tching by James Tissot for
ᴅᴍᴏɴᴅ and ᴊᴜʟᴇs ᴅᴇ ɢᴏɴᴄᴏᴜʀᴛ (May 26, December 17), *Renée Mauperin*
ꜰꜱ: G. Charpentier et Cie, 1884
ne Elisha Whittelsey Collection, The Elisha Whittelsey Fund, 1964   64.597.3

Alfred Austin 1835

_____

_____

_____

_____

_____

Tears are summer showers to the soul.
  Alfred Austin

●●●

Walt Whitman 1819
Helen Waddell 1889
Gladys Schmitt 1909

_____

_____

_____

_____

I am as bad as the worst, but, thank
God, I am as good as the best.

   Walt Whitman

●●●●●●●●●●●

WALT WHITMAN (May 31)
Walt Whitman inciting the bird of freedom
to soar.
Illustration by Max Beerbohm for
The Poets' Corner
London: William Heinemann, 1904
The Elisha Whittelsey Collection, The Elisha Whittelsey
Fund, by exchange, 1955   55.650.3

JUNE 1

John Masefield 1878
John Drinkwater 1882

_____

_____

_____

_____

The days that make us happy make us wise.

John Masefield

JUNE 2

Marquis de Sade 1740
Thomas Hardy 1840
Barbara Pym 1913

_____

_____

_____

_____

A lover without indiscretion is no lover at all.

Thomas Hardy

THOMAS HARDY (June 2)
Portrait of Thomas Hardy, No. 1 (detail)
Etching by William Strang, n.d.
Rogers Fund, 1918   18.45.14

JUNE 3

Sydney Smith 1771
Robert Hillyer 1895
Allen Ginsberg 1926

I think breakfast so pleasant because no one is conceited before one o'clock.

Sydney Smith

JUNE 4

Jeremy Belknap 1744

A clear statement is the strongest argument.

English proverb

JUNE 5

Edmond Duranty 1833
John Maynard Keynes 1883
Margaret Drabble 1939

I do not know which makes a man more conservative– to know nothing but the present, or nothing but the past.

John Maynard Keynes

MOND DURANTY (June 5)
arcoal and chalk drawing by Hilaire-Germain-Edgar Degas, ca. 1879
gers Fund, 1919   19.51.9a

Pierre Corneille 1606
Aleksandr Pushkin 1799
Thomas Mann 1875

Instead of leading the world, America
appears to have resolved to buy it.

Thomas Mann

R. D. Blackmore 1825
Elizabeth Bowen 1899
Gwendolyn Brooks 1917

Charles Reade 1814
Marguerite Yourcenar 1903

ALEKSANDR PUSHKIN (June 6)
Engraving by Louis Marcoussis, n.d.
Print Collection, The New York Public Library
Astor, Lenox and Tilden Foundations

Meeting people unlike oneself does not
enlarge one's outlook; it only confirms
one's idea that one is unique.

Elizabeth Bowen

Make 'em laugh; make 'em cry; make
'em wait.

Charles Reade

•••

John Howard Payne 1791
Marcia Davenport 1903

———————————————

———————————————

———————————————

———————————————

Be it ever so humble, there's no place like home.

John Howard Payne

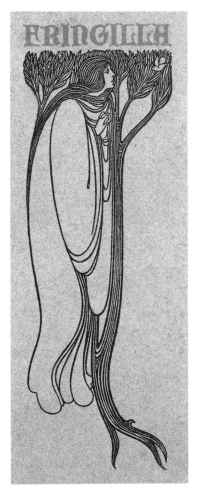

Cover design by Will Bradley for
R. D. BLACKMORE (June 7),
Fringilla, or Tales in Verse
Cleveland: Burrows Brothers Co., 1895
Gift of Fern Bradley Dufner, The Will Bradley
Collection, 1952   52.625.106

•••

Edwin Arnold 1832
Louis Couperus 1863
Saul Bellow 1915

———————————————

———————————————

———————————————

———————————————

Pity makes the world soft to the weak and noble for the strong.

Edwin Arnold

JUNE 11

Ben Jonson 1572
Irving Howe 1920
William Styron 1925

_____

_____

_____

_____

Calumnies are answered best with silence.

Ben Jonson

JUNE 12

Harriet Martineau 1802
Charles Kingsley 1819
Anne Frank 1929

_____

_____

_____

_____

Men who pass most comfortably through the world are those who possess good digestions and hard hearts.

Harriet Martineau

JUNE 13

Fanny Burney 1752
W. B. Yeats 1865
Dorothy L. Sayers 1893

_____

_____

_____

_____

To avoid what is common, without adopting what is unnatural, must limit the ambition of the vulgar herd of authors. . . .

Fanny Burney

Harriet Beecher Stowe 1811
René Char 1907
Jerzy Kosinski 1933

_____

_____

_____

_____

A man builds a house in England with
the expectation of living in it and leav-
ing it to his children; while we shed our
houses in America as easily as a snail
his shell.

Harriet Beecher Stowe

◆◆◆◆◆◆◆◆◆◆◆

Illustration by Warwick Goble for
CHARLES KINGSLEY (June 12),
The Water Babies
London: Macmillan & Co., 1924

Gift of Miss Fairchild Bowler, 1965   65.518.31

JUNE 15

Thomas Randolph 1605
William McFee 1881

Elysia Hunt

_____

_____

_____

_____

The world belongs to the Enthusiast
who keeps cool.

    William McFee

Tom reading his Bible.
Wood engraving after George Cruikshank
for HARRIET BEECHER STOWE (June 14),
Uncle Tom's Cabin
London: John Cassell, 1852

JUNE 16

Erich Segal 1937
Joyce Carol Oates 1938

_____

_____

_____

_____

We are stimulated to emotional re-
sponse not by works that confirm our
sense of the world, but by works that
challenge it.

    Joyce Carol Oates

JUNE 17

John Wesley 1703
Carl Van Vechten 1880
John Hersey 1914

_____

_____

_____

_____

Though I am always in haste, I am
never in a hurry.

John Wesley

JUNE 18

Ivan Goncharov 1812
Philip Barry 1896
Sylvia Porter 1913

_____

_____

_____

_____

It is a trick among the dishonest to offer
sacrifices that are not needed, or not
possible, to avoid making those that
are required.

Ivan Goncharov

JUNE 19

Blaise Pascal 1623
C. H. Spurgeon 1834

_____

_____

_____

_____

What a difficult thing it is to ask someone's advice on a matter without coloring his judgment by the way in which
we present our problem.

Blaise Pascal

JUNE **20**

Lillian Hellman 1905

_____

_____

_____

_____

Since when do you have to agree with
people to defend them from injustice?

Lillian Hellman

9/75

G Braque

JUNE 21

Jean-Paul Sartre 1905
Mary McCarthy 1912
Françoise Sagan 1935

_____

_____

_____

_____

People with bad consciences always
fear the judgment of children.

Mary McCarthy

◆◆◆◆◆◆◆◆◆◆◆

L'Iris. Color lithograph by Georges Braque
for RENE CHAR (June 14), *Lettera amorosa*,
1963
Gift of Mrs. Maurice E. Blin, 1977   1977.582.2

JUNE 22

H. Rider Haggard 1856
Erich Maria Remarque 1897
Gilbert Highet 1906

_____

_____

_____

_____

What is politics but persuading the
public to vote for this and support that
and endure these for the promise of
those?

Gilbert Highet

JUNE 23

Giambattista Vico 1668
Jean Anouilh 1910

_____

_____

_____

_____

Everything in France is a pretext for a
good dinner.

Jean Anouilh

Ambrose Bierce 1842
John Ciardi 1916

_____

_____

_____

_____

_____

In each human heart are a tiger, a pig,
an ass, and a nightingale; diversity
of character is due to their unequal
activity.

Ambrose Bierce

Etching by Albert Gleizes for
BLAISE PASCAL (June 19),
Pensées sur l'homme et Dieu
Casablanca: J. Klein, Editions
de la Cigogne, 1950

George Orwell 1903

Bernard Berenson 1865
Pearl Buck 1892
Laurie Lee 1914

At 50, everyone has the face he deserves.

George Orwell

Engraving by Moreau le Jeune for
JEAN JACQUES ROUSSEAU (June 28),
Julie ou la nouvelle Héloïse, 1774
Harris Brisbane Dick Fund, 1917   17.3.3181

It is no simple matter to pause in the midst of one's maturity, when life is full of function, to examine what are the principles which control that functioning.

Pearl Buck

JUNE 27

Lafcadio Hearn 1850
Paul Laurence Dunbar 1872
Frank O'Hara 1926

_____

_____

_____

_____

The soul doth view its awful self alone,
Ere sleep comes down to soothe the
weary eyes.

Paul Laurence Dunbar

JUNE 28

Jean Jacques Rousseau 1712
Luigi Pirandello 1867
Maureen Howard 1930

_____

_____

_____

_____

To write a good love-letter, you ought
to begin without knowing what you
mean to say, and to finish without
knowing what you have written.

Jean Jacques Rousseau

JUNE 29

Giacomo Leopardi 1798
Antoine de Saint-Exupéry 1900

_____

_____

_____

_____

Love does not consist in gazing at each
other but in looking outward in the
same direction.

Antoine de Saint-Exupéry

John Gay 1685
Georges Duhamel 1884
Czelaw Milosz 1911

Courtesy is not dead – it has merely
taken refuge in Great Britain.

Georges Duhamel

Watercolor by Edmond Dulac for
NATHANIEL HAWTHORNE (July 4), *Tanglewood Tales*, 1919
Spencer Collection, The New York Public Library
Astor, Lenox and Tilden Foundations

JULY 1

Gottfried Wilhelm Leibniz 1646
George Sand 1804

Meagan Johnston

_____

_____

_____

_____

Discouragement seizes us only when
we can no longer count on chance.

George Sand

Illustration by JEAN COCTEAU (July 5),
hand-colored by M. B. Armington,
for *Le livre blanc*
Paris: Editions du Signe, 1930
Gift of Lincoln Kirstein, 1952   52.546.14

JULY 2

Friedrich Gottlieb Klopstock 1724
Hermann Hesse 1877

_____

_____

_____

_____

Each man's life represents a road
toward himself. . . .

Hermann Hesse

···

Franz Kafka 1883
Tom Stoppard 1937

_____

_____

_____

_____

···

Nathaniel Hawthorne 1804

_____

_____

_____

_____

Illustration by Alexander Calder for
JEAN DE LA FONTAINE (July 8),
Selected Fables
New York: Quadrangle Press, 1948
John B. Turner Fund, 1966   66.757.4

Love has as few problems as
motor car. The only prob-
ems are the driver, the pas-
engers, and the road.

Franz Kafka

Punishment of a miser,–to pay the
drafts of his heir in his tomb.

Nathaniel Hawthorne

JULY 5

Jean Cocteau 1889

_____

_____

_____

_____

Tact consists in knowing how far
to go too far.

Jean Cocteau

JULY 6

Françoise Mallet-Joris 1930

_____

_____

_____

_____

In doubtful matters courage may
do much; in desperate, patience

French saying

Illustration by Antonio Frasconi for
PABLO NERUDA (July 12), *Bestiary*
New York: Harcourt, Brace & World, 1965
Gift of Albert TenEyck Gardner, 1966   66.531

JULY 7

Leon Feuchtwanger 1884
Robert Heinlein 1907

Bretton Udvardy

_____

_____

_____

An elephant– a mouse built to
government specifications.

Robert Heinlein

Etching with aquatint by Jacques Villon for
MAX JACOB (July 12), *A poèmes rompus*. Paris: Louis Broder, 1960

JULY 8

Jean de la Fontaine 1621
Alec Waugh 1898
Shirley Ann Grau 1929

_____

_____

_____

_____

How wealthy the gods would be if we
remembered the promises we made
when we were in danger.

Jean de la Fontaine

JULY 9

Ann Radcliffe 1764
Barbara Cartland 1901

_____

_____

_____

_____

A well-informed mind . . . is the best
security against the contagion of folly
and of vice.

Ann Radcliffe

JULY 10

Frederick Marryat 1792
Marcel Proust 1871

_____

_____

_____

_____

When we have understood, we hear in
retrospect.

Marcel Proust

JULY II

Jean-François Marmontel 1723
E. B. White 1899
Frederick Buechner 1926

Jackie Zurborg

_____

_____

_____

_____

One of the most time-consuming
things is to have an enemy.

E. B. White

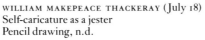

WILLIAM MAKEPEACE THACKERAY (July 18)
Self-caricature as a jester
Pencil drawing, n.d.

JULY I2

Henry D. Thoreau 1817
Max Jacob 1876
Pablo Neruda 1904

_____

_____

_____

_____

It takes two to speak the truth – one to
speak, and another to hear.

Henry D. Thoreau

Isaac Babel 1894
Wole Soyinka 1934

F. R. Leavis 1895
Irving Stone 1903
Isaac Bashevis Singer 1904

A simile must be as precise as a slide rule and as natural as the smell of dill. . . .

Isaac Babel

Woodcut (detail) for
PETRARCH (July 20), *Li triumphi, soneti & canzone*
Venice: Bartholomeo Zanni, 1508
Rogers Fund, 1917   17.43.1

If you keep saying things are going to be bad you have a good chance of being a prophet.

Isaac Bashevis Singer

JULY 15

Clement Moore 1779
Gavin Maxwell 1914
Iris Murdoch 1919

Philosophy . . . means looking at things which one takes for granted and suddenly seeing that they are very odd indeed.

Iris Murdoch

JULY 16

Mary Baker Eddy 1821

Two points of danger beset mankind; namely, making sin seem either too large or too small.

Mary Baker Eddy

JULY 17

S. Y. Agnon 1888
Erle Stanley Gardner 1889
Christina Stead 1902

Along come the scientists and make the words of our fathers into folklore.

S. Y. Agnon

JULY 18

William Makepeace Thackeray 1811
Clifford Odets 1906
Yevgeny Yevtushenko 1933

_____

_____

_____

_____

If a man's character is to be abused, say what you will, there's nobody like a relation to do the business.

William Makepeace Thackeray

JULY 19

Vladimir Mayakovsky 1893
A. J. Cronin 1896

_____

_____

_____

_____

. . . amiability and good temper do not come easily when one is hungry. . . .

A. J. Cronin

JULY 20

Petrarch 1304
Thomas Berger 1924

_____

_____

_____

_____

To be able to say how much you love is to love but little.

Petrarch

JULY 21

Hart Crane 1899
Ernest Hemingway 1899

Etching with aquatint by Jean Bruller for
ANDRE MAUROIS (July 26), *Deux fragments
d'une histoire universelle, 1992*
Paris: Paul Hartmann, 1929

The Elisha Whittelsey Collection,
The Elisha Whittelsey Fund, 1966   66.556.8

Real seriousness in regard to writing is
one of two absolute necessities. The
other, unfortunately, is talent.

Ernest Hemingway

JULY 22

Emma Lazarus 1849
Stephen Vincent Benét 1898
Alan Moorehead 1910

There is a time, after every revolution,
when men have to sit down, take stock,
and decide on what sort of government
they mean to live under.

Stephen Vincent Benét

JULY 23

•••

Coventry Patmore 1823
Raymond Chandler 1888

_____

_____

_____

_____

He didn't know the right people.
That's all a police record means.

Raymond Chandler

JULY 24

•••

Alexandre Dumas, *père* 1802
Lord Dunsany 1878
Robert Graves 1895

_____

_____

_____

_____

There's no money in poetry, but then
there's no poetry in money either.

Robert Graves

JULY 25

•••

Elias Canetti 1905

_____

_____

_____

_____

Learning is the art of ignoring.

Elias Canetti

JULY 26

George Bernard Shaw 1856
André Maurois 1885
Aldous Huxley 1894

_____

_____

_____

_____

Married people should never travel
together: they blame one another for
everything that goes wrong. . . .

George Bernard Shaw

••••••••••••

GEORGE BERNARD SHAW (July 26)
Mr. George Bernard Shaw – Capitalist
Pen, black ink and watercolor
drawing by Max Beerbohm, n.d.

JULY 27

Thomas Campbell 1777
Hilaire Belloc 1870
Elizabeth Hardwick 1916

_____

_____

_____

_____

_____

Coming events cast their shadows
before.

Thomas Campbell

JULY 28

Gerard Manley Hopkins 1844
Beatrix Potter 1866
Malcolm Lowry 1909

I am soft sift
In an hourglass – at the wall
Fast, but mined with a motion, a drift
And it crowds and it combs to the
fall. . . .

Gerard Manley Hopkins

••••••••••••

Heathcliff under the tree.
Wood engraving by Fritz Eichenberg
for EMILY BRONTË (July 30),
Wuthering Heights, 1943

John B. Turner Fund, 1967   67.624.3

JULY 29

Booth Tarkington 1869
Don Marquis 1878
Stanley Kunitz 1905

So long as we can lose happiness, we
possess some.

Booth Tarkington

JULY 30

Giorgio Vasari 1511
Emily Brontë 1818
Thorstein Veblen 1857

The corset is, in economic theory, sub-
stantially a mutilation, undergone for
the purpose of lowering the subject's
vitality and rendering her permanently and obviously unfit for work.

Thorstein Veblen

JULY 31

Helena Blavatsky 1831

_____

_____

_____

_____

We live in an age of prejudice, dissimulation and paradox . . . ever struggling between our honest convictions and fear of that cruelest of tyrants— PUBLIC OPINION.

Helena Blavatsky

AUGUST 1

Herman Melville 1819
Rose Macaulay 1881

_____

_____

_____

_____

Life's a voyage that's homeward bound.

Herman Melville

AUGUST 2

Ernest Dowson 1867
James Baldwin 1924

_____

_____

_____

_____

What is the use of speech? Silence were fitter:
Lest we should still be wishing things unsaid.

Ernest Dowson

Rupert Brooke 1887
P. D. James 1920
Leon Uris 1924

_____

_____

_____

_____

_____

The worst friend and enemy is but
Death.

Rupert Brooke

Pen and ink drawing by Rockwell Kent for
HERMAN MELVILLE (August 1), *Moby Dick*
Chicago: The Lakeside Press, 1930

Percy Bysshe Shelley 1792
Walter Pater 1839
Knut Hamsun 1859

_____

_____

_____

_____

_____

Life may change, but it may fly not;
Hope may vanish, but can die not;
Truth be veiled, but still it burneth;
Love repulsed,—but it returneth.

   Percy Bysshe Shelley

Etching with hand coloring by Henri
Boutet for GUY DE MAUPASSANT (August 5)
"Une partie de campagne," from *Contes choisi.*
Paris: L'Académie des Beaux Livres, 1891–9

AUGUST 5

Guy de Maupassant 1850
Conrad Aiken 1889

The bed comprehends our whole life,
for we were born in it, we live in it,
and we shall die in it.

Guy de Maupassant

AUGUST 6

François Fénelon 1651
Alfred, Lord Tennyson 1809
Paul Claudel 1868

Knowledge comes, but wisdom
lingers.

Alfred, Lord Tennyson

ALFRED, LORD TENNYSON (August 6)
Albumin photograph by
Oscar Gustav Rejlander, ca. 1863
Harris Brisbane Dick Fund, 1941   41.21.21

AUGUST 7

Joseph Rodman Drake 1795
Frederic William Farrar 1831

_____

_____

_____

_____

There is only one real failure in life that is possible, and that is, not to be true to the best one knows.

Frederic William Farrar

AUGUST 8

Charles A. Dana 1819
Sara Teasdale 1884
Marjorie Kinnan Rawlings 1896

_____

_____

_____

_____

I make the most of all that comes,
    And the least of all that goes.

Sara Teasdale

AUGUST 9

Izaak Walton 1593
John Dryden 1631
Philip Larkin 1922

_____

_____

_____

_____

Beware the fury of a patient man.

John Dryden

AUGUST 10

Laurence Binyon 1869
Witter Bynner 1881
Jorge Amado 1912

_____

_____

_____

_____

A man's language is an unerring index of his nature.

Laurence Binyon

PAUL CLAUDEL (August 6)
Lithograph by Raoul Dufy for
Ode jubilaire pour le six-centième anniversaire de la mort de Dante
Paris: Editions de la Nouvelle Revue Française, 1921

The Elisha Whittelsey Collection,
The Elisha Whittelsey Fund, 1966   66.542.8

AUGUST 11

Octave Feuillet 1821
Hugh MacDiarmid 1892
Angus Wilson 1913

_____

_____

_____

_____

Gossip is the henchman of rumor and scandal.

Octave Feuillet

AUGUST 12

•••

Robert Southey 1774
Mary Roberts Rinehart 1876
Frank Swinnerton 1884

_____

_____

_____

_____

_____

Live as long as you may, the first
twenty years are the longest half of
your life.

Robert Southey

AUGUST 13

•••

Nikolaus Lenau 1802

Wood engraving by the Dalziel Brothers
after A. B. Houghton for
ROBERT BUCHANAN (August 18),
"A Scottish Eclogue," from *North Coast
and Other Poems*
London: George Routledge and Sons, 1868
Gift of Sinclair Hamilton, 1965   65.629.10

_____

_____

_____

_____

_____

He is not the best statesman who is the
greatest doer, but he who sets others
doing with the greatest success.

Anonymous

AUGUST 14

John Galsworthy 1867
Frederic Raphael 1931

_____

_____

_____

_____

The beginnings and endings of all
human undertakings are untidy, the
building of a house, the writing of a
novel, the demolition of a bridge, and,
eminently, the finish of a voyage.

John Galsworthy

AUGUST 15

Sir Walter Scott 1771
Thomas De Quincey 1785
Edna Ferber 1887

_____

_____

_____

_____

Too much rest is rust.

Sir Walter Scott

AUGUST 16

Jules Laforgue 1860
T. E. Lawrence 1888
Ted Hughes 1930

_____

_____

_____

_____

Those who dream by night . . . wake in
the day to find that it was vanity: but
the dreamers of the day are dangerous
men, for they may act their dreams
with open eyes, to make it possible.

T. E. Lawrence

AUGUST 17

Wilfred Scawen Blunt 1840
John Hawkes 1925
V. S. Naipaul 1932

He who has once been happy is for aye
Out of destruction's reach.

Wilfred Scawen Blunt

AUGUST 18

Robert Buchanan 1841
Elsa Morante 1918
Alain Robbe-Grillet 1922

Like all the centuries and the millennia
that have preceded it on earth, the new
century also observes the well-known,
immobile principle of historical
dynamics: power to some, servitude to
others.

Elsa Morante

AUGUST 19

Pierre Jean de Béranger 1780
Ogden Nash 1902
James Gould Cozzens 1903

What divides men is less a difference in
ideas than a likeness in pretensions.

Pierre Jean de Béranger

AUGUST 20

Edgar A. Guest 1881
Salvatore Quasimodo 1901
Jacqueline Susann 1921

To Meddowes

Ye have been fresh and green,
  Ye have been fill'd with flowers:
And ye the walks have been
  Where maids have spent their houres.

You have beheld, how they
  With wicker arks did come
To kisse and beare away
  The richer cowslips home.

Yave heard them sweetly sing,
  And seen them in a round:
Each virgin, like a spring,
  With hony-succkles crown'd

But now, we see, none here,
  Whose silv'rie feet did tread,
And with disheuell'd haire,
  Adorn'd this smoother mead.

Like vnthrifts, hauing spent
  Yovr stock, and needy grown,
Y'are left here to lament
  Yovr poore estates, alone

He started to sing as he tackled the
    thing
  That couldn't be done, and he did it.

Edgar A. Guest

Illustration by Edwin Austin Abbey for ROBERT HERRICK (August 24),
"To Meadowes," from *Selection from the Poetry of Robert Herrick*
London: Sampson Low-Marston, 1882

Gift of Mitchell Kennerley, 1923

AUGUST 21

Jules Michelet 1798
X. J. Kennedy 1929

_____

_____

_____

_____

It is the general rule, that all superior
men inherit the elements of superiority
from their mothers.

Jules Michelet

AUGUST 22

Dorothy Parker 1893
René Wellek 1903
Ray Bradbury 1920

_____

_____

_____

_____

And this is the sum of a lasting lore:
Scratch a lover, and find a foe.

Dorothy Parker

AUGUST 23

Edgar Lee Masters 1868
Arthur Adamov 1908

_____

_____

_____

_____

To this generation I would say:
Memorize some bit of verse of truth
or beauty.

Edgar Lee Masters

Le Hibou.

Woodcut by Raoul Dufy for
GUILLAUME APOLLINAIRE (August 26), *Le bestiaire*. Paris: Deplanche, 1911

Harris Brisbane Dick Fund, 1926   26.92.30

Robert Herrick 1591
Jean Rhys 1894
Jorge Luis Borges 1899

If little labour, little are our gaines:
Man's fortune's are according to his
    paines.

Robert Herrick

AUGUST **25**

Bret Harte 1836
Brian Moore 1921

_____

_____

_____

_____

_____

One big vice in a man is apt to keep out
a great many smaller ones.

Bret Harte

Drawing by Reginald Marsh for
THEODORE DREISER (August 27), *An American Tragedy*, ca. 1934
Print Collection, The New York Public Library, Astor, Lenox and Tilden Foundations

AUGUST 26

Guillaume Apollinaire 1880
Christopher Isherwood 1904
Julio Cortázar 1914

_____

_____

_____

_____

The nights of Paris all drink gin
And fall asleep with their streetlights
   on.

Guillaume Apollinaire

AUGUST 27

Georg Wilhelm Friedrich Hegel 1770
Theodore Dreiser 1871
C. S. Forester 1899

_____

_____

_____

_____

It is easier to discover a deficiency in
individuals, in states, and in Provi-
dence, than to see their real import
and value.

Georg Wilhelm Friedrich Hegel

AUGUST 28

Johann Wolfgang von Goethe 1749
Bruno Bettelheim 1903
Robertson Davies 1913

_____

_____

_____

_____

Mediocrity has no greater consolation
than in the thought that genius is not
immortal.

Johann Wolfgang von Goethe

AUGUST 29

John Locke 1632
Oliver Wendell Holmes 1809
Thom Gunn 1929

_____

_____

_____

_____

Science is a first-rate piece of furniture for a man's upper chamber, if he has common sense on the ground floor.

Oliver Wendell Holmes

AUGUST 30

Mary Shelley 1797
Paul Hazard 1878
John Gunther 1901

_____

_____

_____

_____

The most indolent person may read a maxim, and ponder on its truth, and be led to meditate, without any violent exertion of mind.

Mary Shelley

AUGUST 31

Théophile Gautier 1811
William Saroyan 1908

_____

_____

_____

_____

All things return to dust
  Save beauty fashioned well;
The bust
  Outlasts the citadel.

Théophile Gautier

SEPTEMBER I

Countess of Blessington 1789
Lydia Sigourney 1791
Edgar Rice Burroughs 1875

_____

_____

_____

_____

Borrowed thoughts, like borrowed
money, only show the poverty of the
borrower.

Countess of Blessington

LE TORO ESPAGNOL

Etching with aquatint by Pablo Picasso for
COMTE DE BUFFON (September 7), *Histoire naturelle*
Print Collection, The New York Public Library, Astor, Lenox and Tilden Foundations

SEPTEMBER 2

Giovanni Verga 1840
Eugene Field 1850
David Daiches 1912

Maria Stockal

Women are by nature fickle, and so are men. . . . Not so with books, for books cannot change. A thousand years hence they are what you find them today, speaking the same words, holding forth the same comfort.

Eugene Field

SEPTEMBER 3

Sarah Orne Jewett 1849
Alison Lurie 1926

As one went to Europe to see the living past, so one must visit Southern California to observe the future.

Alison Lurie

SEPTEMBER 4

Chateaubriand 1768
Antonin Artaud 1896
Richard Wright 1908

As soon as a true thought has entered our mind, it gives a light which makes us see a crowd of other objects which we have never perceived before.

Chateaubriand

SEPTEMBER 5

Victorien Sardou 1831
Arthur Koestler 1905
Frank Yerby 1916

SEPTEMBER 6

Henry Seidel Canby 1878
Mario Praz 1896

LUDOVICO ARIOSTO (September 8)
Engraving for *Orlando furioso*
Venice: Gio. Andrea Valvassore, 1556
Harris Brisbane Dick Fund, 1937   37.37.12

When all is said and done, one loves one's country not *because* of this or that, but rather, in spite of it all.

Arthur Koestler

The American imagination releases itself very easily in the short story— and has done so since the beginning of our national history.

Henry Seidel Canby

SEPTEMBER 7

Comte de Buffon 1707
Edith Sitwell 1887
Taylor Caldwell 1900

_____

_____

_____

_____

_____

I am patient with stupidity, but not with those who are proud of it.

Edith Sitwell

SEPTEMBER 8

Ludovico Ariosto 1474
Alfred Jarry 1873
Siegfried Sassoon 1886

_____

_____

_____

_____

_____

Fortune, who gives and takes away all other human blessings, has no power over courage.

Ludovico Ariosto

SEPTEMBER 9

Leo Tolstoy 1828
Mary Austin 1868
Cesare Pavese 1908

_____

_____

_____

_____

_____

When one has made a mistake, one says: "Next time I shall really know what to do." What one should say is: "I already know what I shall really do next time."

Cesare Pavese

SEPTEMBER 10

Franz Werfel 1890

_____

_____

_____

_____

_____

. . . the only advantage that the hunted
has in this world is that he can never be
the hunter.

Franz Werfel

Color woodcut by E. Othon Friesz for
PIERRE DE RONSARD (September 11), *Poèmes*. Paris: Gonin Frères, 1934
Spencer Collection, The New York Public Library, Astor, Lenox and Tilden Foundations

Pierre de Ronsard 1524
O. Henry 1862
D. H. Lawrence 1885

H. L. Mencken 1880
Louis MacNeice 1907

J. Fenimore Cooper

The modern pantheist not only sees god in everything, he takes photographs.

D. H. Lawrence

JAMES FENIMORE COOPER (September 15)
Steel engraving by W. E. Marshall
after a design by C. L. Elliott for
The Cooper Vignettes
New York: James G. Gregory, 1862

The Elisha Whittelsey Collection,
The Elisha Whittelsey Fund, 1964   64.667

A cynic is a man who, when he smells flowers, looks around for a coffin.

H. L. Mencken

SEPTEMBER 13

Sherwood Anderson 1876
J. B. Priestley 1894
Roald Dahl 1916

Andrew Kennedy

_____

_____

_____

_____

Living in an age of advertisement, we
are perpetually disillusioned.

J. B. Priestley

SEPTEMBER 14

Michel Butor 1926
Kate Millett 1934

_____

_____

_____

_____

Whatever the "real" differences between the sexes may be, we are not
likely to know them until the sexes are
treated differently, that is alike.

Kate Millett

SEPTEMBER 15

François, duc de la Rochefoucauld
1613
James Fenimore Cooper 1789
Agatha Christie 1890

_____

_____

_____

_____

Old people like to give good advice,
as solace for no longer being able to
provide bad examples.

François, duc de la Rochefoucauld

SEPTEMBER 16

Lord Bolingbroke 1678
Frans Sillanpää 1888
Gwen Bristow 1903

Marie Sevigny

Misu

_____

_____

_____

Pride defeats its own end, by bringing
the man who seeks esteem and rever-
ence into contempt.

Gwen Bristow

SEPTEMBER 17

William Carlos Williams 1883
Frank O'Connor 1903

_____

_____

_____

_____

I have discovered that most of
the beauties of travel are due to
the strange hours we keep to see
them. . . .

William Carlos Williams

SEPTEMBER 18

James Shirley 1596
Samuel Johnson 1709

_____

_____

_____

_____

We are inclined to believe those we do
not know, because they have never
deceived us.

Samuel Johnson

William Golding 1911

Upton Sinclair 1878
Donald Hall 1928

Woodcut for SAVONAROLA (September 21),
Predica del arte del bene morire
Florence: Antonio Tubini & Co., ca. 1500
Harris Brisbane Dick Fund, 1925   25.30.95

. . . the shape of a society must depend
on the ethical nature of the individual
and not on any political system however apparently logical or respectable.

William Golding

It is difficult to get a man to understand
something when his salary depends
upon his not understanding it.

Upton Sinclair

Savonarola 1452
Edmund Gosse 1849
H. G. Wells 1866

_____

_____

_____

_____

_____

Lord Chesterfield 1694
Alice Meynell 1847

_____

_____

_____

_____

_____

Illustration by Hugh Thomson for
ELIZABETH GASKELL (September 29),
Cranford
London and New York: Macmillan & Co.,
1891
Museum Accession, 1921   21.36.81

'Hush, ladies! if you please, hush!'

Moral indignation is jealousy
with a halo.

H. G. Wells

Patience is a most necessary
quality for business: many a
man would rather you heard his
story than granted his request.

Lord Chesterfield

William Golding 1911

Upton Sinclair 1878
Donald Hall 1928

Woodcut for SAVONAROLA (September 21),
Predica del arte del bene morire
Florence: Antonio Tubini & Co., ca. 1500
Harris Brisbane Dick Fund, 1925   25.30.95

. . . the shape of a society must depend
on the ethical nature of the individual
and not on any political system however apparently logical or respectable.

William Golding

It is difficult to get a man to understand
something when his salary depends
upon his not understanding it.

Upton Sinclair

SEPTEMBER 23

Walter Lippmann 1889

_____

_____

_____

_____

Propaganda is that branch of lying which often deceives your friends without ever deceiving your enemies.

Walter Lippmann

SEPTEMBER 24

Horace Walpole 1717
A. P. Herbert 1890
F. Scott Fitzgerald 1896

_____

_____

_____

_____

An author ought to write for the youth of his own generation, the critic of the next, and the schoolmaster of ever afterwards.

F. Scott Fitzgerald

SEPTEMBER 25

William Faulkner 1897

_____

_____

_____

_____

There's no such thing as bad whiskey. Some whiskeys just happen to be better than others. But a man shouldn't fool with booze until he's fifty; then he's a damn fool if he doesn't.

William Faulkner

T. S. Eliot 1888

_____

_____

_____

_____

The immature poet imitates; the
mature poet plagiarizes.

T. S. Eliot

Don Quixote and Sancho Panza.
Drawing by Honoré Daumier for MIGUEL DE CERVANTES (September 29), *Don Quixote*, n.d.
Rogers Fund, 1927   27.152.1

SEPTEMBER 27

Grazia Deledda 1875
William Empson 1906
Louis Auchincloss 1917

_____

_____

_____

_____

New York has absolutely everything
today except the past.

Louis Auchincloss

SEPTEMBER 28

Prosper Mérimée 1803
Elmer Rice 1892

Todd MacDonald

_____

_____

_____

In history I only love the anecdotes.

Prosper Mérimée

SEPTEMBER 29

Miguel de Cervantes 1547
Elizabeth Gaskell 1810

_____

_____

_____

_____

A little credulity helps one on through
life very smoothly.

Elizabeth Gaskell

SEPTEMBER 30

Truman Capote 1924
W. S. Merwin 1927
Elie Wiesel 1928

_____

_____

_____

_____

Venice is like eating an entire box of
chocolate liqueurs in one go.

Truman Capote

OCTOBER 1

William Beckford 1760
Louis Untermeyer 1885

_____

_____

_____

_____

Give me the heart to fight and lose.

Louis Untermeyer

OCTOBER 2

Wallace Stevens 1879
Roy Campbell 1901
Graham Greene 1904

_____

_____

_____

_____

Sentimentality – that's what we call
the sentiment we don't share.

Graham Greene

OCTOBER 3

Alain Fournier 1886
Thomas Wolfe 1900
Gore Vidal 1925

The surest cure for vanity is loneliness.

Thomas Wolfe

Engraving for DENIS DIDEROT (October 5),
Les bijoux indiscrets
Monomotapa (Paris? 1748?)

Rare Books and Manuscripts Division, The New York
Public Library, Astor, Lenox and Tilden Foundations

OCTOBER 4

Damon Runyon 1884
Brendan Gill 1914

My boy . . . always try to rub up
against money, for if you rub up
against money long enough, some
of it may rub off on you.

Damon Runyon

Denis Diderot 1713

Caroline Gordon 1895

Pithy sentences are like sharp nails which force truth upon our memory.

Denis Diderot

Etching by Auguste Gérardin for
FRANCISQUE SARCEY (October 8),
Paris vivant. Le théâtre
Paris: Société Artistique du Livre Illustré,
1893

Harris Brisbane Dick Fund, 1930   30.103.9

You must plough with such oxen as you have.

English proverb

OCTOBER 7

James Whitcomb Riley 1849

_____

_____

_____

_____

Oh! the old swimmin' hole! When I
    last saw the place,
The scenes was all changed, like the
    change in my face.

James Whitcomb Riley

OCTOBER 8

Francisque Sarcey 1827
John Hay 1838
John Cowper Powys 1872

_____

_____

_____

_____

True luck consists not in holding the
    best of the cards at the table:
Luckiest he who knows just when to
    rise and go home.

John Hay

OCTOBER 9

Bruce Catton 1899
Leopold Senghor 1906

_____

_____

_____

_____

A nation built on the idea that all
men – *all men* – are of equal worth and
equal rights summons every one of its
citizens to a life-long commitment to
put that idea into practical effect.

Bruce Catton

OCTOBER 10

Ivo Andrić 1892
Harold Pinter 1930

_____

_____

_____

_____

One way of looking at speech is to say
it is a constant stratagem to cover
nakedness.

Harold Pinter

OCTOBER 11

François Mauriac 1885

_____

_____

_____

_____

We know well only what we are
deprived of.

François Mauriac

OCTOBER 12

George W. Cable 1844
Eugenio Montale 1896

_____

_____

_____

_____

That gardening is best . . . which best
ministers to man's felicity with least
disturbance of nature's freedom.

George W. Cable

Thomas Haynes Bayly 1797

Woodcut by Aristide Maillol for
VIRGIL (October 15), *Die Eclogen Virgils.* Weimar: Cranach Press, 1926
Harris Brisbane Dick Fund, 1928   28.12

Absence makes the heart grow
fonder. . . .

Thomas Haynes Bayly

OCTOBER 14

Katherine Mansfield 1888
e. e. cummings 1894
Hannah Arendt 1906

———————————————

———————————————

———————————————

———————————————

———————————————

. . . roses are the only flowers that
impress people at garden-parties;
the only flowers that everybody is
certain of knowing.

Katherine Mansfield

⟡⟡⟡⟡⟡⟡⟡⟡⟡⟡

Color lithograph by Jim Dine for
OSCAR WILDE (October 16),
The Picture of Dorian Gray
London: Petersburg Press, 1968

John B. Turner Fund, 1969   69.564

OCTOBER 15

Virgil 70 B.C.
Friedrich Nietzsche 1844
C. P. Snow 1905

Whoever fights monsters should see to it that in the process he does not become a monster. And when you look long into an abyss, the abyss also looks into you.

Friedrich Nietzsche

OCTOBER 16

Oscar Wilde 1854
Eugene O'Neill 1888
Günter Grass 1927

A poet can survive everything but a misprint.

Oscar Wilde

OCTOBER 17

Elinor Glyn 1864
Nathanael West 1903
Arthur Miller 1915

The man who makes an appearance in the business world, the man who creates personal interest, is the man who gets ahead. Be liked and you will never want.

Arthur Miller

OCTOBER 18

Thomas Love Peacock 1785
Henri Bergson 1859

_____

_____

_____

_____

A book that furnishes no quotations is, *me judice*, no book– it is a plaything.

Thomas Love Peacock

OCTOBER 19

Sir Thomas Browne 1605
Lewis Mumford 1895
John Le Carré 1931

_____

_____

_____

_____

Layer upon layer, past times preserve themselves in the city until life itself is finally threatened with suffocation; then, in sheer defense, modern man invents the museum.

Lewis Mumford

OCTOBER 20

Arthur Rimbaud 1854
John Dewey 1859
Frederic Dannay 1905

Rob Schellenberg

_____

_____

_____

To find out what one is fitted to do and to secure an opportunity to do it is the key to happiness.

John Dewey

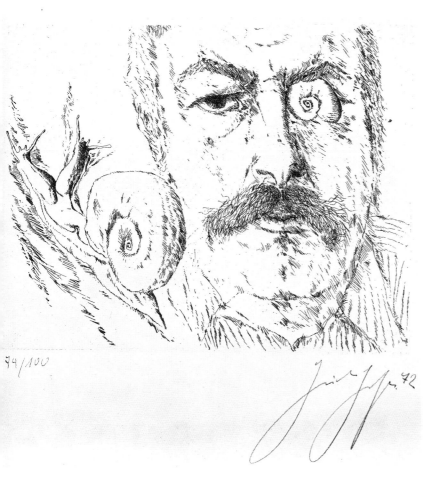

74/100

GÜNTER GRASS (October 16). Self-portrait I. Etching, 1972
Print Collection, The New York Public Library, Astor, Lenox and Tilden Foundations

Samuel Taylor Coleridge 1772
Alphonse de Lamartine 1790
Maureen Duffy 1933

_____

_____

_____

_____

Nought cared this body for wind or
    weather,
When youth and I lived in't together.

Samuel Taylor Coleridge

OCTOBER **22**

Ivan Bunin 1870
Doris Lessing 1919

_____

_____

_____

_____

It is only in love and in war that we escape from the sleep of necessity, the cage of ordinary life, to a state where every day is high adventure. . . .

Doris Lessing

Illustration by Alexander Calder for
SAMUEL TAYLOR COLERIDGE (October 21), *The Rime of the Ancient Mariner*
New York: Reynal and Hitchcock, 1946
The Elisha Whittelsey Collection, The Elisha Whittelsey Fund, 1969   69.589.7

OCTOBER 23

Restif de la Bretonne 1734
Robert Bridges 1844
J. Michael Crichton 1942

___

___

___

___

The heart of youth is reached through the senses; the senses of age are reached through the heart.

Restif de la Bretonne

OCTOBER 24

Moss Hart 1904
Denise Levertov 1923

___

___

___

___

Poor people know poor people, and rich people know rich people. It is one of the few things La Rochefoucauld did not say, but then La Rochefoucauld never lived in the Bronx.

Moss Hart

OCTOBER 25

Thomas Babington Macaulay 1800
John Berryman 1914
Anne Tyler 1941

___

___

___

___

A great writer is the friend and benefactor of his readers.

Thomas Babington Macaulay

OCTOBER 26

John Arden 1930

_____

_____

_____

_____

. . . an unwillingness to dwell upon unpleasant situations that do not immediately concern us is a general human trait, and recognition of it need imply neither cynicism nor despair.

John Arden

OCTOBER 27

Dylan Thomas 1914
Sylvia Plath 1932

_____

_____

_____

_____

Fear most
For ever of all not the wolf in his baaing
hood
Nor the tusked prince, in the ruttish
farm, at the rind
And mire of love, but the Thief as
meek as the dew.

Dylan Thomas

OCTOBER 28

Evelyn Waugh 1903

_____

_____

_____

_____

I have come to the conclusion that there is no such thing as normality. That is what makes story-telling such an absorbing task, the attempt to reduce to order the anarchic raw materials of life.

Evelyn Waugh

James Boswell 1740
Jean Giraudoux 1882

He who praises everybody, praises nobody.

James Boswell

❦❦❦❦❦❦❦❦❦

Etching by Jacques Mauny for
JEAN GIRAUDOUX (October 29),
Amica America
Paris: Aux Editions Emile-Paul Frères,
1928
The Elisha Whittelsey Collection,
The Elisha Whittelsey Fund, 1964   64.611

OCTOBER 30

Richard Brinsley Sheridan 1751
Paul Valéry 1871
Ezra Pound 1885

_____

_____

_____

_____

Believe that story false that ought not
to be true.

Richard Brinsley Sheridan

PAUL VALERY (October 30)
Frontispiece etching by
Edmund Marie for *Choses tues*
Paris: Les Editions Lapina, 1930

The Elisha Whittelsey Collection,
The Elisha Whittelsey Fund, 1964   64.618.2

OCTOBER 31

John Keats 1795
Axel Munthe 1857
Dick Francis 1920

_____

_____

_____

_____

The excellency of every art is its inten-
sity, capable of making all disagree-
ables evaporate.

John Keats

NOVEMBER 1

Stephen Crane 1871
Sholem Asch 1880
Edmund Blunden 1896

_____

_____

_____

_____

Preaching is fatal to art in literature.

Stephen Crane

⟩⟩⟩⟩⟩⟩⟩⟩⟩⟩

Illustration by Winslow Homer for
WILLIAM CULLEN BRYANT (November 3),
The Story of the Fountain
New York: D. Appleton & Co., 1872
Harris Brisbane Dick Fund, 1933   33.72.1

NOVEMBER 2

•••

Benjamin Perley Poore 1820
Martin Flavin 1883

——————————————

——————————————

——————————————

——————————————

Life proceeds at an uneven pace, in jerks and spurts, like growing plants and children.

Martin Flavin

NOVEMBER 3

•••

William Cullen Bryant 1794
André Malraux 1901

——————————————

——————————————

——————————————

——————————————

Our heritage is composed of all the voices that can answer our questions.

André Malraux

NOVEMBER 4

•••

G. E. Moore 1873
Will Rogers 1879

——————————————

——————————————

——————————————

——————————————

Everybody is ignorant, only on different subjects.

Will Rogers

Ella Wheeler Wilcox 1850
James Elroy Flecker 1884
Thomas Flanagan 1923

_____

_____

_____

_____

Feast, and your halls are crowded;
Fast, and the world goes by.

Ella Wheeler Wilcox

Wood engraving after Otto Speckter for
FRITZ REUTER (November 7), *Hanne Nüte
un de lütte Pudel*
Wismar und Ludwigslust: Verlag der
Hinstorff'schen Hofbuchhandlung, 1865
Harris Brisbane Dick Fund, 1932   32.20.5

Wood engraving by Alexander Anderson
for MARK AKENSIDE (November 9),
The Pleasures of the Imagination
Portland: Thomas B. Waite & Co., 1807
Harris Brisbane Dick Fund, 1934   34.1.3

Colley Cibber 1671
James Jones 1921

_____

_____

_____

_____

Who fears to offend takes the first step
to please.

Colley Cibber

The social evening. Etching with aquatint by Thomas Rowlandson for
OLIVER GOLDSMITH (November 10), *The Vicar of Wakefield*. London: R. Ackermann, 1817

NOVEMBER 7

Fritz Reuter 1810
Leonora Speyer 1872
Albert Camus 1913

Stephen Sykora

Art and revolt will die only with the
last man.

Albert Camus

NOVEMBER 8

Margaret Mitchell 1900
Peter Weiss 1916

. . . the world can forgive practically
anything except people who mind
their own business.

Margaret Mitchell

NOVEMBER 9

Mark Akenside 1721
Ivan Turgenev 1818
Anne Sexton 1928

I share no man's opinions; I have my
own.

Ivan Turgenev

NOVEMBER 10

Martin Luther 1483
Oliver Goldsmith 1730
Johann von Schiller 1759

Adam Gauthier

Mark Bykowski

Hope like the gleaming taper's light
Adorns and cheers our way,
And still as darker grows the night
Emits a brighter ray.

Oliver Goldsmith

NOVEMBER 11

Fyodor Dostoevsky 1821
Kurt Vonnegut, Jr. 1922

Malgorzata Klimowiz

In order to act wisely it is not enough
to be wise.

Fyodor Dostoevsky

NOVEMBER 12

Elizabeth Cady Stanton 1815
Roland Barthes 1915

Whenever the skilled hands and cul-
tured brain of women have made the
battle of life easier for man, he has
readily pardoned her sound judgment
and proper self-assertion.

Elizabeth Cady Stanton

Saint Augustine of Hippo 354
Robert Louis Stevenson 1850
William Gibson 1914

_____

_____

_____

_____

_____

If you want a person's faults, go to those who love him. They will not tell you, but they know.

Robert Louis Stevenson

ANTICHRISTVS.

Woodcut by Hans Cranach for
MARTIN LUTHER (November 10), *Antithesis figurata vitae Christi et Antichristi*
Wittenberg: J. Grunenberg, 1521

Rogers Fund, 1919   19.49.1

Frederick Jackson Turner 1861
John Patrick 1911

Chris Agterbos

_____

_____

_____

_____

I admit disappointment but not defeat.

John Patrick

NOVEMBER 15

Franklin P. Adams 1881
Marianne Moore 1887
Sacheverell Sitwell 1897

_____

_____

_____

_____

_____

The best part of the fiction in many
novels is the notice that the characters
are all purely imaginary.

Franklin P. Adams

Lithograph by Antoni Clavé for VOLTAIRE
(November 21), *Candide; ou, l'optimisme*
Paris: Chez Jean Porson, 1948(?)

NOVEMBER 16

George S. Kaufman 1889
Michael Arlen 1895
Chinua Achebe 1930

_____

_____

_____

_____

. . . when a coward sees a man he can
beat he becomes hungry for a fight.

Chinua Achebe

NOVEMBER 17

George Grote 1794
Archibald Lampman 1861

_____

_____

_____

_____

An idle brain is the devil's workshop.

English proverb

NOVEMBER 18

W. S. Gilbert 1836
Wyndham Lewis 1882
Jacques Maritain 1882

_____

_____

_____

_____

Oh, don't the days seem lank and long,
When all goes right and nothing goes
    wrong?
And isn't your life extremely flat
With nothing whatever to grumble at?

W. S. Gilbert

NOVEMBER 19

Allen Tate 1899

_____

_____

_____

_____

Man is a creature that in the long run
has got to believe in order to know, and
to know in order to do.

Allen Tate

NOVEMBER 20

Thomas Chatterton 1752
Selma Lagerlöf 1858
Nadine Gordimer 1923

_____

_____

_____

_____

. . . there will always be those who
cannot live with themselves at the ex-
pense of fullness of life for others.

Nadine Gordimer

NOVEMBER 21

Voltaire 1694
Arthur Quiller-Couch 1863
Marilyn French 1929

_____

_____

_____

_____

The secret of being a bore is to tell
everything.

Voltaire

George Eliot 1819
George Gissing 1857
André Gide 1869

_____

_____

_____

_____

Blessed is the man who, having
nothing to say, abstains from giving
us wordy evidence of the fact.

   George Eliot

   ❦❦❦❦❦❦❦❦❦❦

Wood engraving by Jules Germain and
L. Petitbarat after Marie Laurencin for
ANDRE GIDE (November 22),
La tentative amoureuse, où le traité du vain désir
Paris: Editions de la Nouvelle Revue
Française, 1921

●●

P. K. Page 1916
Paul Célan 1920

_____

_____

_____

_____

Forty is the old age of youth; fifty is
the youth of old age.

French proverb

The baptism. Drawing by William Hogarth
for LAURENCE STERNE (November 24),
Tristram Shandy, 1760

Berg Collection, The New York Public Library
Astor, Lenox and Tilden Foundations

●●

Benedict de Spinoza 1632
Laurence Sterne 1713
Frances Hodgson Burnett 1849

_____

_____

_____

_____

When the heart flies out before the
understanding, it saves the judgement
a world of pains.

Laurence Sterne

NOVEMBER 25

Lope de Vega 1562
H. Granville-Barker 1877
Leonard Woolf 1880

_____

_____

_____

_____

Anyone can be a barbarian; it requires a terrible effort to be or remain a civilized man.

Leonard Woolf

NOVEMBER 26

William Cowper 1731
Eugène Ionesco 1912

_____

_____

_____

_____

A nose that can see is worth two that sniff.

Eugène Ionesco

NOVEMBER 27

James Agee 1909
Gail Sheehy 1937

_____

_____

_____

_____

The English instinctively admire any man who has no talent and is modest about it.

James Agee

John Bunyan 1628
William Blake 1757
Alberto Moravia 1907

_____

_____

_____

_____

_____

How do you know but ev'ry Bird that
    cuts the airy way,
Is an immense world of delight, clos'd
    by your senses five?

William Blake

Engraving with hand coloring by
WILLIAM BLAKE (November 28) for "The
Sick Rose," from *Songs of Experience*, 1825
Rogers Fund, 1917   17.10.39

NOVEMBER 29

Louisa May Alcott 1832
C. S. Lewis 1898
Carlo Levi 1902

Marc Huot

The Future is something which everyone reaches at the rate of sixty minutes an hour, whatever he does, whoever he is.

C. S. Lewis

NOVEMBER 30

Sir Philip Sidney 1554
Jonathan Swift 1667
Mark Twain 1835

A man who is ostentatious of his modesty is twin to the statue that wears a figleaf.

Mark Twain

Engraving after Crispin van de Passe for SIR PHILIP SIDNEY (November 30), *L'arcadie de la Comtesse de Pembrok, 1624–5*

MARK TWAIN (November 30)
Oil on canvas by Charles Noël Flagg, 1890

Gift of Ellen Earle Flagg, 1917   17.96

Anna Comnena 1083
Rex Stout 1886

Jasmine Politeski

_____

_____

_____

_____

My theory is that people who don't like
detective stories are anarchists.

Rex Stout

DECEMBER 2

David Masson 1822
Joseph P. Lash 1909

_____

_____

_____

_____

. . . the measure of the value of any
work of fiction . . . is the worth of the
speculations, the philosophy, on
which it rests, and which has entered
into the conception of it.

David Masson

DECEMBER 3

Joseph Conrad 1857

_____

_____

_____

_____

Vanity plays lurid tricks with our
memory.

Joseph Conrad

DECEMBER 4

Thomas Carlyle 1795
Samuel Butler 1835
Rainer Maria Rilke 1875

_____

_____

_____

_____

The oldest books are still only just out
to those who have not read them.

Samuel Butler

Christina Rossetti 1830
Joan Didion 1934
Calvin Trillin 1935

_____

_____

_____

_____

_____

All things that pass
Are wisdom's looking-glass.

Christina Rossetti

Aquatint by Donald Saff for
RAINER MARIA RILKE (December 4),
Sonnets to Orpheus
New York: Martin Gallery, n.d.

John B. Turner Fund, 1966   66.688(8)

DECEMBER 6

Joyce Kilmer 1886
Osbert Sitwell 1892
Gunnar Myrdal 1898

Lisa Popek

I am most fond of talking and thinking; that is to say, talking first and thinking afterwards.

Osbert Sitwell

DECEMBER 7

Johan Huizinga 1872
Willa Cather 1873
Joyce Cary 1888

Marcin Siembab

There are only two or three human stories, and they go on repeating themselves as fiercely as if they had never happened before.

Willa Cather

THOMAS CARLYLE (December 4)
Pen and wash drawing by
Walter Greaves, n.d.

The Elisha Whittelsey Collection,
The Elisha Whittelsey Fund, 1950   50.605.34

DECEMBER 8

Horace 65 B.C.
James Thurber 1894
Delmore Schwartz 1913

Carolyn Selby

A host is like a general: it takes a
mishap to reveal his genius.

Horace

JOHN MILTON (December 9). Oil on canvas by Robert Streater, n.d.
Gift of Mrs. Wheeler Smith, 1908   08.237.1

DECEMBER 9

John Milton 1608
Joel Chandler Harris 1848

Carol Agterbos-Squire

_____

_____

_____

_____

The mind is its own place, and in itself
Can make a heav'n of hell, a hell of
    heav'n.

John Milton

DECEMBER 10

Emily Dickinson 1830
Nelly Sachs 1891
William Plomer 1903

_____

_____

_____

_____

_____

Life is so rotatory that the wilderness
falls to each, sometime.

Emily Dickinson

Brush and black-ink drawing by
André Dunoyer de Segonzac for
GUSTAVE FLAUBERT (December 12),
L'éducation sentimentale, ca. 1922

Bequest of Miss Adelaide Milton de Groot (1876–1967),
1967   67.187.33

DECEMBER 11

Alfred de Musset 1810
Aleksandr Solzhenitsyn 1918

A great writer is, so to speak, a second
government in his country. And for
that reason no regime has ever loved
great writers, only minor ones.

Aleksandr Solzhenitsyn

DECEMBER 12

Gustave Flaubert 1821
John Osborne 1929

Of all the icy blasts that blow on love, a
request for money is the most chilling
and havoc-wreaking.

Gustave Flaubert

DECEMBER 13

Heinrich Heine 1797
Kenneth Patchen 1911
Ross Macdonald 1915

Experience is a good school, but the
fees are high.

Heinrich Heine

Lithograph by Jules Pascin for
HEINRICH HEINE (December 13), *Aus den Memoiren des Herrn von Schnabelewopsky*
Berlin: Paul Cassirer, 1910
Harris Brisbane Dick Fund, 1929   29.10.1

Shirley Jackson 1919

I believe all women, but especially
housewives, tend to think in lists. . . .

Shirley Jackson

DECEMBER 15

Maxwell Anderson 1888
Muriel Rukeyser 1913
Edna O'Brien 1930

_____

_____

_____

_____

_____

. . . the more frugal and honest you are
the less power you need.

Maxwell Anderson

"She is tolerable"

Drawing by Hugh Thompson for
JANE AUSTEN (December 16), *Pride and Prejudice*, 1893–94
Spencer Collection, The New York Public Library, Astor, Lenox and Tilden Foundations

DECEMBER 16

Jane Austen 1775
V. S. Pritchett 1900
Margaret Mead 1901

_____

_____

_____

_____

What dreadful weather . . . it keeps one
in a continual state of inelegance.

Jane Austen

DECEMBER 17

John Greenleaf Whittier 1807
Jules de Goncourt 1830
Ford Madox Ford 1873

_____

_____

_____

_____

For of all sad words of tongue or pen,
The saddest are these: "It might have
been!"

John Greenleaf Whittier

DECEMBER 18

Saki 1870
Christopher Fry 1907

_____

_____

_____

_____

In baiting a mouse trap with cheese,
always leave room for the mouse.

Saki

Italo Svevo 1861
Jean Genêt 1910

_____

_____

_____

_____

_____

To achieve harmony in bad taste is the height of elegance.

Jean Genêt

Snow-Bound.

Had been to us companionship,
And, in our lonely life, had grown
To have an almost human tone.
As night drew on, and, from the crest
Of wooded knolls that ridged the west,
The sun, a snow-blown traveller, sank
From sight beneath the smothering bank,
We piled, with care, our nightly stack
Of wood against the chimney-back, —

Wood engraving by W. J. Linton after
a design by Harry Fenn for
JOHN GREENLEAF WHITTIER
(December 17), *Snow-Bound*
Boston: Fields, Osgood & Co., 1869
Rogers Fund, 1919   19.44.34

T. F. Powys 1875
Hortense Calisher 1911

_____

_____

_____

_____

Although a man can always gain more, his joy in his gains is never more at the last than at the first transaction.

T. F. Powys

DECEMBER 21

Benjamin Disraeli 1804
Anthony Powell 1905
Heinrich Böll 1917

_____

_____

_____

_____

Next to knowing when to seize an
opportunity, the most important thing
in life is to know when to forgo an
advantage.

Benjamin Disraeli

DECEMBER 22

Jean Racine 1639
Edwin Arlington Robinson 1869
Kenneth Rexroth 1905

_____

_____

_____

_____

Small crimes always precede great
ones. Never have we seen timid
innocence pass suddenly to extreme
licentiousness.

Jean Racine

DECEMBER 23

Charles Sainte-Beuve 1804
Giuseppe di Lampedusa 1896
Robert Bly 1926

_____

_____

_____

_____

There are people whose watch stops
at a certain hour and who remain
permanently at that age.

Charles Sainte-Beuve

DECEMBER 24

George Crabbe 1754
Matthew Arnold 1822
Juan Ramón Jiménez 1881

_____

_____

_____

_____

One's age should be tranquil, as childhood should be playful. Hard work at either extremity of life seems out of place.

Matthew Arnold

DECEMBER 25

William Collins 1721
Rebecca West 1892
Carlos Castaneda 1931

_____

_____

_____

_____

All the world over, the most good-natured find enjoyment in those who miss trains or sit down on frozen pavements.

Rebecca West

DECEMBER 26

Thomas Gray 1716
Henry Miller 1891
Mao Tse-Tung 1893

_____

_____

_____

_____

Teach me to love and to forgive,
Exact my own defects to scan,
What others are, to feel, and know
myself a Man.

Thomas Gray

ENRY MILLER (December 26). Self-portrait in pencil with pen and India ink
Wrapper for typescript of *Remember to Remember*, 1946
erg Collection, The New York Public Library, Astor, Lenox and Tilden Foundations

Louis Bromfield 1896
Wilfrid Sheed 1930

Ashley King

_____

_____

_____

_____

It may be that we have to lose that
knowledge and understanding which
children have and then perhaps it
comes back to us through living experience and wisdom.

Louis Bromfield

DECEMBER 28

Antoine Furetière 1619
Pio Baroja 1872

_____

_____

_____

_____

. . . everything of a dangerous character has its antidote; love and prostitution, freedom and prisons.

Pio Baroja

DECEMBER 29

Morley Roberts 1857
Robert Ruark 1915
William Gaddis 1922

Jason Carter

_____

_____

_____

When there is no proof of guilt, there may well be none of innocence.

Morley Roberts

DECEMBER 30

Rudyard Kipling 1865
Stephen Leacock 1869

_____

_____

_____

_____

. . . the average patient looks upon the average doctor very much as the noncombatant looks upon the troops fighting on his behalf. The more trained men there are between his body and the enemy the better.

Rudyard Kipling

DECEMBER 31

James T. Fields 1817
Holbrook Jackson 1874

How sweet and gracious, even in
   common speech,
Is that fine sense which men call
   Courtesy!

James T. Fields

Illustration by RUDYARD KIPLING
(December 30) for
"The Cat That Walked by Himself,"
from *Just So Stories for Children*
London: Macmillan & Co., 1902

Rogers Fund, 1974   1974.617.6

List of Writers

Abé, Kobo   Mar. 7
Abercrombie, Lascelles   Jan. 9
Achebe, Chinua   Nov. 16
Adamov, Arthur   Aug. 23
Adams, Franklin P.   Nov. 15
Adams, Henry   Feb. 16
Adams, Richard   May 9
Addison, Joseph   May 1
Agee, James   Nov. 27
Agnon, S. Y.   July 17
Aiken, Conrad   Aug. 5
Akenside, Mark   Nov. 9
Alarcón, Pedro Antonio de   Mar. 10
Albee, Edward   Mar. 12
Alcott, Louisa May   Nov. 29
Aldrich, Bess Streeter   Feb. 17
Aleichem, Sholem   Feb. 18
Alfieri, Vittorio   Jan. 16
Alger, Horatio   Jan. 13
Algren, Nelson   Mar. 28
Allingham, Margery   May 20
Amado, Jorge   Aug. 10
Amis, Kingsley   April 16
Andersen, Hans Christian   April 2
Anderson, Maxwell   Dec. 15
Anderson, Sherwood   Sept. 13
Andrić, Ivo   Oct. 10
Angelou, Maya   April 4
Anouilh, Jean   June 23
Apollinaire, Guillaume   Aug. 26
Arden, John   Oct. 26
Arendt, Hannah   Oct. 14
Ariosto, Ludovico   Sept. 8

Arlen, Michael   Nov. 16
Arnold, Edwin   June 10
Arnold, Matthew   Dec. 24
Artaud, Antonin   Sept. 4
Asch, Sholem   Nov. 1
Asimov, Isaac   Jan. 2
Auchincloss, Louis   Sept. 27
Auden, W. H.   Feb. 21
Augustine of Hippo, Saint   Nov. 13
Aurelius, Marcus   April 26
Austen, Jane   Dec. 16
Austin, Alfred   May 30
Austin, Mary   Sept. 9

Babel, Isaac   July 13
Bacon, Francis   Jan. 22
Bagehot, Walter   Feb. 3
Baldwin, James   Aug. 2
Balzac, Honoré de   May 20
Bang, Herman   April 20
Barbusse, Henri   May 17
Baring-Gould, Sabine   Jan. 28
Barnes, Margaret Ayer   April 8
Baroja, Pio   Dec. 28
Barrie, J. M.   May 9
Barry, Philip   June 18
Barthelme, Donald   April 7
Barthes, Roland   Nov. 12
Baudelaire, Charles   April 9
Baum, L. Frank   May 15
Baum, Vicki   Jan. 24
Bayly, Thomas Haynes   Oct. 13

Beaumarchais, Pierre   Jan. 24
Beauvoir, Simone de   Jan. 9
Beckett, Samuel   April 13
Beckford, William   Oct. 1
Behan, Brendan   Feb. 9
Belknap, Jeremy   June 4
Belloc, Hilaire   July 27
Bellow, Saul   June 10
Benét, Stephen Vincent   July 22
Bentham, Jeremy   Feb. 15
Béranger, Pierre Jean de   Aug. 19
Berenson, Bernard   June 26
Berger, Thomas   July 20
Bergson, Henri   Oct. 18
Berkeley, George   Mar. 12
Bernanos, Georges   Feb. 20
Berne, Eric   May 10
Berryman, John   Oct. 25
Betjeman, John   April 6
Bettelheim, Bruno   Aug. 28
Bierce, Ambrose   June 24
Binyon, Laurence   Aug. 10
Birrell, Augustine   Jan. 19
Blackmore, R. D.   June 7
Blackmur, R. P.   Jan. 21
Blake, William   Nov. 28
Blavatsky, Helena   July 31
Blessington, Countess of   Sept. 1
Blunden, Edmund   Nov. 1
Blunt, Wilfred Scawen   Aug. 17
Bly, Robert   Dec. 23
Bolingbroke, Lord   Sept. 16
Böll, Heinrich   Dec. 21

Bombeck, Erma   Feb. 21
Borges, Jorge Luis   Aug. 24
Boswell, James   Oct. 29
Bowen, Elizabeth   June 7
Bowra, C. M.   April 8
Boyle, Kay   Feb. 19
Bradbury, Ray   Aug. 22
Braine, John   April 13
Brecht, Bertolt   Feb. 10
Breton, André   Feb. 18
Bridges, Robert   Oct. 23
Brillat-Savarin, Anthelme   April 1
Bristow, Gwen   Sept. 16
Bromfield, Louis   Dec. 27
Brontë, Anne   Jan. 17
Brontë, Charlotte   April 21
Brontë, Emily   July 30
Brooke, Rupert   Aug. 3
Brooks, Gwendolyn   June 7
Brooks, Van Wyck   Feb. 16
Browne, Sir Thomas   Oct. 19
Browning, Elizabeth Barrett   Mar. 6
Browning, Robert   May 7
Bryant, William Cullen   Nov. 3
Buber, Martin   Feb. 8
Buchanan, Robert   Aug. 18
Buck, Pearl   June 26
Buechner, Frederick   July 11
Buffon, Comte de   Sept. 7
Bulwer-Lytton, Edward   May 25
Bunin, Ivan   Oct. 22
Bunyan, John   Nov. 28
Burgess, Anthony   Feb. 25
Burke, Edmund   Jan. 12
Burnett, Frances Hodgson   Nov. 24
Burney, Fanny   June 13
Burns, Robert   Jan. 25
Burroughs, Edgar Rice   Sept. 1

Burroughs, William   Feb. 5
Burton, Richard F.   Mar. 19
Butler, Samuel   Feb. 7 (1612)
Butler, Samuel   Dec. 4 (1835)
Butor, Michel   Sept. 14
Bynner, Witter   Aug. 10
Byron, Lord   Jan. 22

Cabell, James Branch   April 14
Cable, George W.   Oct. 12
Caine, Hall   May 14
Caldwell, Taylor   Sept. 7
Calisher, Hortense   Dec. 20
Campbell, Roy   Oct. 2
Campbell, Thomas   July 27
Campion, Thomas   Feb. 12
Camus, Albert   Nov. 7
Canby, Henry Seidel   Sept. 6
Canetti, Elias   July 25
Capote, Truman   Sept. 30
Carlyle, Thomas   Dec. 4
Carroll, Lewis   Jan. 27
Cartland, Barbara   July 9
Cary, Alice   April 26
Cary, Joyce   Dec. 7
Casanova, Giacomo   April 5
Castaneda, Carlos   Dec. 25
Cather, Willa   Dec. 7
Catton, Bruce   Oct. 9
Cela, Camilo José   May 11
Célan, Paul   Nov. 23
Céline, Louis-Ferdinand   May 27
Cervantes, Miguel de   Sept. 29
Chandler, Raymond   July 23
Char, René   June 14
Chardin, Pierre Teilhard de   May 1
Chase, Stuart   Mar. 8

Chateaubriand   Sept. 4
Chatterton, Thomas   Nov. 20
Cheever, John   May 27
Chekhov, Anton   Jan. 29
Chesterfield, Lord   Sept. 22
Chesterton, G. K.   May 29
Christie, Agatha   Sept. 15
Ciardi, John   June 24
Cibber, Colley   Nov. 6
Cicero   Jan. 3
Claudel, Paul   Aug. 6
Cocteau, Jean   July 5
Coleridge, Samuel Taylor   Oct. 21
Colette   Jan. 28
Collins, Wilkie   Jan. 8
Collins, William   Dec. 25
Comnena, Anna   Dec. 1
Conrad, Joseph   Dec. 3
Conway, Moncure Daniel   Mar. 17
Cooper, James Fenimore   Sept. 15
Coppard, A. E.   Jan. 4
Corneille, Pierre   June 6
Cortázar, Julio   Aug. 26
Couperus, Louis   June 10
Cowper, William   Nov. 26
Cozzens, James Gould   Aug. 19
Crabbe, George   Dec. 24
Crane, Hart   July 21
Crane, Stephen   Nov. 1
Crébillon, Prosper Jolyot de   Jan. 13
Creeley, Robert   May 21
Crichton, J. Michael   Oct. 23
Croce, Benedetto   Feb. 25
Cronin, A. J.   July 19
Crouse, Russel   Feb. 20
cummings, e. e.   Oct. 14
Cunninghame Graham, R. B.   May 24

Dahl, Roald   Sept. 13
Daiches, David   Sept. 2
Dana, Charles A.   Aug. 8
Dannay, Frederic   Oct. 20
D'Annunzio, Gabriele   Mar. 12
Dante Alighieri   May 14
Darwin, Charles   Feb. 12
Daudet, Alphonse   May 13
Davenport, Marcia   June 9
Davies, Robertson   Aug. 28
Davis, Richard Harding   April 18
de la Mare, Walter   April 25
Deledda, Grazia   Sept. 27
d'Epinay, Madame   Mar. 11
De Quincey, Thomas   Aug. 15
Desmoulins, Camille   Mar. 2
de Vere, Aubrey   Jan. 10
Dewey, John   Oct. 20
Dibdin, Charles   Mar. 4
Dickens, Charles   Feb. 7
Dickinson, Emily   Dec. 10
Diderot, Denis   Oct. 5
Didion, Joan   Dec. 5
Dillard, Annie   April 30
Dinesen, Isak   April 17
Disraeli, Benjamin   Dec. 21
Doctorow, E. L.   Jan. 6
Dodge, M. M.   Jan. 26
Dos Passos, John   Jan. 14
Dostoevsky, Fyodor   Nov. 11
Dowson, Ernest   Aug. 2
Doyle, Arthur Conan   May 22
Drabble, Margaret   June 5
Drake, Joseph Rodman   Aug. 7
Dreiser, Theodore   Aug. 27
Drinkwater, John   June 1
Dryden, John   Aug. 9

Du Bois, W. E. B.   Feb. 23
Duffy, Maureen   Oct. 21
du Gard, Roger Martin   Mar. 23
Duhamel, Georges   June 30
Dumas *père*, Alexandre   July 24
du Maurier, Daphne   May 13
Dunbar, Paul Laurence   June 27
du Nerval, Gérard   May 22
Dunsany, Lord   July 24
Duranty, Edmond   June 5
Durrell, Gerald   Jan. 7
Durrell, Lawrence   Feb. 27
Dürrenmatt, Friedrich   Jan. 5

Echegaray, José   April 19
Eddy, Mary Baker   July 16
Einstein, Albert   Mar. 14
Eliot, George   Nov. 22
Eliot, T. S.   Sept. 26
Ellis, Havelock   Feb. 2
Ellmann, Richard   Mar. 15
Emerson, Ralph Waldo   May 25
Empson, William   Sept. 27
Endo, Shusaku   Mar. 27
Enright, D. J.   Mar. 11
Eucken, Rudolf   Jan. 5

Farjeon, Eleanor   Feb. 13
Farrar, Frederic William   Aug. 7
Faulkner, William   Sept. 25
Feiffer, Jules   Jan. 26
Fénelon, François   Aug. 6
Ferber, Edna   Aug. 15
Ferlinghetti, Lawrence   Mar. 24

Feuchtwanger, Leon   July 7
Feuillet, Octave   Aug. 11
Feydeau, Ernest   Mar. 16
Fichte, Johann   May 19
Field, Eugene   Sept. 2
Fielding, Henry   April 22
Fields, James T.   Dec. 31
Fisher, Dorothy Canfield   Feb. 17
Fitzgerald, F. Scott   Sept. 24
Flanagan, Thomas   Nov. 5
Flaubert, Gustave   Dec. 12
Flavin, Martin   Nov. 2
Flecker, James Elroy   Nov. 5
Fleming, Ian   May 28
Fogazzaro, Antonio   Mar. 25
Fontenelle, Bernard   Feb. 11
Ford, Ford Madox   Dec. 17
Ford, Paul Leicester   Mar. 23
Forester, C. S.   Aug. 27
Forster, E. M.   Jan. 1
Foscolo, Ugo   Feb. 6
Fournier, Alain   Oct. 3
Fowles, John   Mar. 31
France, Anatole   April 16
Francis, Dick   Oct. 31
Frank, Anne   June 12
Freeman, Douglas Southall   May 16
French, Marilyn   Nov. 21
Freneau, Philip   Jan. 2
Freud, Sigmund   May 6
Friedan, Betty   Feb. 4
Fromm, Erich   Mar. 23
Frost, Robert   Mar. 26
Fry, Christopher   Dec. 18
Fuller, Henry B.   Jan. 9
Fuller, Margaret   May 23
Fuller, Roy   Feb. 11
Furetière, Antoine   Dec. 28

Gaddis, William   Dec. 29
Galdós, Benito Pérez   May 10
Galsworthy, John   Aug. 14
Galt, John   May 2
Gardner, Erle Stanley   July 17
Garnett, David   Mar. 9
Garrick, David   Feb. 19
Gaskell, Elizabeth   Sept. 29
Gautier, Théophile   Aug. 31
Gay, John   June 30
Genêt, Jean   Dec. 19
Gibbon, Edward   May 8
Gibson, William   Nov. 13
Gide, André   Nov. 22
Gilbert, W. S.   Nov. 18
Gill, Brendan   Oct. 4
Ginsberg, Allen   June 3
Giraudoux, Jean   Oct. 29
Gissing, George   Nov. 22
Glasgow, Ellen   April 22
Glyn, Elinor   Oct. 17
Godwin, William   Mar. 3
Goethe, Johann Wolfgang von   Aug. 28
Gogol, Nikolai   Mar. 31
Golding, William   Sept. 19
Goldoni, Carlo   Feb. 25
Goldsmith, Oliver   Nov. 10
Goncharov, Ivan   June 18
Goncourt, Edmond de   May 26
Goncourt, Jules de   Dec. 17
Gordimer, Nadine   Nov. 20
Gordon, Caroline   Oct. 6
Gorky, Maxim   Mar. 28
Gosse, Edmund   Sept. 21
Grahame, Kenneth   Mar. 8
Granville-Barker, H.   Nov. 25
Grass, Günter   Oct. 16

Grau, Shirley Ann   July 8
Graves, Robert   July 24
Gray, Thomas   Dec. 26
Green, Paul   Mar. 17
Greene, Graham   Oct. 2
Greer, Germaine   Jan. 29
Gregory, Lady   Mar. 15
Grimm, Jacob   Jan. 4
Grimm, Wilhelm   Feb. 24
Grote, George   Nov. 17
Guest, Edgar A.   Aug. 20
Guiney, Louise Imogen   Jan. 7
Güiraldes, Ricardo   Feb. 13
Gunn, Thom   Aug. 29
Gunther, John   Aug. 30

Haggard, H. Rider   June 22
Hale, Edward Everett   April 3
Hall, Donald   Sept. 20
Hamsun, Knut   Aug. 4
Hardwick, Elizabeth   July 27
Hardy, Thomas   June 2
Harris, Joel Chandler   Dec. 9
Hart, Moss   Oct. 24
Harte, Bret   Aug. 25
Hawkes, John   Aug. 17
Hawthorne, Nathaniel   July 4
Hay, John   Oct. 8
Hazard, Paul   Aug. 30
Hazlitt, William   April 10
Hazzard, Shirley   Jan. 30
Hearn, Lafcadio   June 27
Hegel, Georg Wilhelm Friedrich   Aug. 27
Heine, Heinrich   Dec. 13
Heinlein, Robert   July 7
Heller, Joseph   May 1

Hellman, Lillian   June 20
Hemingway, Ernest   July 21
Henry, O.   Sept. 11
Herbert, A. P.   Sept. 24
Herbert, George   April 3
Herrick, Robert   Aug. 24
Hersey, John   June 17
Hesse, Hermann   July 2
Hibbert, Christopher   Mar. 5
Highet, Gilbert   June 22
Highsmith, Patricia   Jan. 19
Hillyer, Robert   June 3
Hobbes, Thomas   April 5
Hofmannsthal, Hugo von   Feb. 1
Hölderlin, Friedrich   Mar. 20
Holmes, Oliver Wendell   Aug. 29
Hood, Thomas   May 23
Hopkins, Gerard Manley   July 28
Horace   Dec. 8
Housman, A. E.   Mar. 26
Howard, Maureen   June 28
Howe, Irving   June 11
Howells, William Dean   Mar. 1
Hughes, Langston   Feb. 1
Hughes, Richard   April 19
Hughes, Ted   Aug. 16
Hugo, Victor   Feb. 26
Huizinga, Johan   Dec. 7
Huxley, Aldous   July 26
Huysmans, Joris-Karl   Feb. 5

Ibsen, Henrik   Mar. 20
Inge, William   May 3
Ionesco, Eugène   Nov. 26
Irving, John   Mar. 2
Irving, Washington   April 3
Isherwood, Christopher   Aug. 26

Jackson, Holbrook   Dec. 31
Jackson, Shirley   Dec. 14
Jacob, Max   July 12
James, Henry   April 15
James, P. D.   Aug. 3
James, William   Jan. 11
Jarrell, Randall   May 6
Jarry, Alfred   Sept. 8
Jaspers, Karl   Feb. 23
Jeffers, Robinson   Jan. 10
Jensen, Johannes V.   Jan. 20
Jerome, Jerome K.   May 2
Jewett, Sarah Orne   Sept. 3
Jiménez, Juan Ramón   Dec. 24
Johnson, Diane   April 28
Johnson, Lionel   Mar. 15
Johnson, Samuel   Sept. 18
Jones, James   Nov. 6
Jonson, Ben   June 11
Joyce, James   Feb. 2

Kafka, Franz   July 3
Kant, Immanuel   April 22
Kaufman, George S.   Nov. 16
Keats, John   Oct. 31
Kennedy, X. J.   Aug. 21
Keynes, John Maynard   June 5
Kierkegaard, Sören   May 5
Kilmer, Joyce   Dec. 6
Kingsley, Charles   June 12
Kinsella, Thomas   May 4
Kipling, Rudyard   Dec. 30
Klopstock, Friedrich Gottlieb   July 2
Koestler, Arthur   Sept. 5
Kosinski, Jerzy   June 14
Kundera, Milan   April 1

Kunitz, Stanley   July 29

La Fontaine, Jean de   July 8
Laforgue, Jules   Aug. 16
Lagerkvist, Pär   May 23
Lagerlöf, Selma   Nov. 20
Lamartine, Alphonse de   Oct. 21
Lamb, Charles   Feb. 10
Lampedusa, Giuseppe di   Dec. 23
Lampman, Archibald   Nov. 17
Landor, Walter Savage   Jan. 30
Lardner, Ring   Mar. 6
Larkin, Philip   Aug. 9
La Rochefoucauld, François,
   duc de   Sept. 15
La Rochelle, Drieu   Jan. 3
Lash, Joseph P.   Dec. 2
Lawrence, D. H.   Sept. 11
Lawrence, T. E.   Aug. 16
Lazarus, Emma   July 22
Leacock, Stephen   Dec. 30
Lear, Edward   May 12
Leavis, F. R.   July 14
Le Carré, John   Oct. 19
Lee, Harper   April 28
Lee, Laurie   June 26
Lee, Manfred B.   Jan. 11
Le Gallienne, Richard   Jan. 20
Leibniz, Gottfried Wilhelm   July 1
Lenau, Nikolaus   Aug. 13
Leopardi, Giacomo   June 29
Lessing, Doris   Oct. 22
Levertov, Denise   Oct. 24
Levi, Carlo   Nov. 29
Lewis, C. Day   April 27
Lewis, C. S.   Nov. 29
Lewis, Sinclair   Feb. 7

Lewis, Wyndham   Nov. 18
Lindsay, Howard   Mar. 29
Linklater, Eric   Mar. 8
Lippmann, Walter   Sept. 23
Llosa, Mario Vargas   Mar. 28
Locke, John   Aug. 29
London, Jack   Jan. 12
Longfellow, Henry Wadsworth   Feb. 27
Longstreet, Stephen   April 18
Lowell, Amy   Feb. 9
Lowell, James Russell   Feb. 22
Lowell, Percival   Mar. 13
Lowell, Robert   Mar. 1
Lowry, Malcolm   July 28
Lubbock, Sir John   April 30
Luce, Clare Boothe   April 10
Lurie, Alison   Sept. 3
Luther, Martin   Nov. 10

Macaulay, Rose   Aug. 1
Macaulay, Thomas Babington   Oct. 25
McCarthy, Mary   June 21
McCullers, Carson   Feb. 19
MacDiarmid, Hugh   Aug. 11
Macdonald, Ross   Dec. 13
McFee, William   June 15
McGinley, Phyllis   Mar. 21
Machiavelli, Niccolò   May 3
McKuen, Rod   April 29
MacLeish, Archibald   May 7
MacNeice, Louis   Sept. 12
Mailer, Norman   Jan. 31
Maimonides, Moses   Mar. 30
Malamud, Bernard   April 26
Mallarmé, Stéphane   Mar. 18
Mallet-Joris, Françoise   July 6
Malraux, André   Nov. 3

Mandelstam, Osip Jan. 15
Mann, Thomas June 6
Mansfield, Katherine Oct. 14
Manzoni, Alessandro Mar. 7
Mao Tse-Tung Dec. 26
Maritain, Jacques Nov. 18
Marivaux, Pierre Feb. 4
Marlowe, Christopher Feb. 6
Marmontel, Jean-François July 11
Márquez, Gabriel García Mar. 6
Marquis, Don July 29
Marryat, Frederick July 10
Marsh, Ngaio April 23
Martineau, Harriet June 12
Marvell, Andrew Mar. 31
Marx, Karl May 5
Masefield, John June 1
Masson, David Dec. 2
Masters, Edgar Lee Aug. 23
Maugham, W. Somerset Jan. 25
Maupassant, Guy de Aug. 5
Mauriac, François Oct. 11
Maurois, André July 26
Maxwell, Gavin July 15
Mayakovsky, Vladimir July 19
Mead, Margaret Dec. 16
Melville, Herman Aug. 1
Mencken, H. L. Sept. 12
Meredith, George Feb. 12
Mérimée, Prosper Sept. 28
Merton, Thomas Jan. 31
Merwin, W. S. Sept. 30
Meynell, Alice Sept. 22
Michelet, Jules Aug. 21
Michener, James Feb. 3
Millay, Edna St. Vincent Feb. 22
Miller, Arthur Oct. 17
Miller, Henry Dec. 26

Millett, Kate Sept. 14
Milne, A. A. Jan. 18
Milosz, Czelaw June 30
Milton, John Dec. 9
Mirandola, Pico della Feb. 24
Mirbeau, Octave Feb. 16
Mishima, Yukio Jan. 14
Mistral, Gabriele April 7
Mitchell, Margaret Nov. 8
Molière Jan. 15
Molnár, Ferenc Jan. 12
Monsarrat, Nicholas Mar. 22
Montagu, Lady Mary Wortley May 26
Montaigne, Michel de Feb. 28
Montale, Eugenio Oct. 12
Montesquieu, Charles Louis
   de Secondat Jan. 18
Moore, Brian Aug. 25
Moore, Clement July 15
Moore, G. E. Nov. 4
Moore, George Feb. 24
Moore, Marianne Nov. 15
Moore, Thomas May 28
Moorehead, Alan July 22
Morante, Elsa Aug. 18
Moravia, Alberto Nov. 28
Morris, William Mar. 24
Morris, Wright Jan. 6
Morrison, Toni Feb. 18
Muir, Edwin May 15
Mumford, Lewis Oct. 19
Munthe, Axel Oct. 31
Murdoch, Iris July 15
Musset, Alfred de Dec. 11
Myrdal, Gunnar Dec. 6

Nabokov, Vladimir April 23

Naipaul, V. S. Aug. 17
Nash, Ogden Aug. 19
Nathan, George Jean Feb. 14
Nathan, Robert Jan. 2
Neruda, Pablo July 12
Newman, John Henry Feb. 21
Nietzsche, Friedrich Oct. 15
Noel, Thomas May 11
Norris, Frank March 5
North, Christopher May 18

Oates, Joyce Carol June 16
O'Brien, Edna Dec. 15
O'Casey, Sean Mar. 30
O'Connor, Flannery Mar. 25
O'Connor, Frank Sept. 17
Odets, Clifford July 18
O'Faolain, Sean Feb. 22
O'Hara, Frank June 27
O'Hara, John Jan. 31
Olsen, Tillie Jan. 14
O'Neill, Eugene Oct. 16
Ortega y Gasset, José May 9
Orton, Joe Jan. 1
Orwell, George June 25
Osborne, John Dec. 12
Ostrovsky, Aleksandr April 12
Otway, Thomas Mar. 3
Ovid Mar. 20
Owen, Wilfred Mar. 18

Packard, Vance May 22
Page, P. K. Nov. 23
Paine, Thomas Jan. 29
Parker, Dorothy Aug. 22
Pascal, Blaise June 19

Vigny, Alfred de   Mar. 27
Virgil   Oct. 15
Voltaire   Nov. 21
Vonnegut, Kurt, Jr.   Nov. 11

Waddell, Helen   May 31
Wain, John   Mar. 14
Walker, Alice   Feb. 9
Wallace, Irving   Mar. 19
Waller, Edmund   Mar. 3
Walpole, Horace   Sept. 24
Walpole, Hugh   Mar. 13
Walton, Izaak   Aug. 9
Warren, Robert Penn   April 24
Wasserman, Jacob   Mar. 10
Waugh, Alec   July 8
Waugh, Evelyn   Oct. 28
Webb, Mary   Mar. 25
Weiss, Peter   Nov. 8
Wellek, René   Aug. 22
Wells, H. G.   Sept. 21
Welty, Eudora   April 13

Werfel, Franz   Sept. 10
Wescott, Glenway   April 11
Wesker, Arnold   May 24
Wesley, John   June 17
West, Nathaniel   Oct. 17
West, Rebecca   Dec. 25
Wharton, Edith   Jan. 24
White, E. B.   July 11
White, Theodore H.   May 6
Whitehead, Alfred North   Feb. 15
Whitman, Walt   May 31
Whittier, John Greenleaf   Dec. 17
Wiesel, Elie   Sept. 30
Wilcox, Ella Wheeler   Nov. 5
Wilde, Oscar   Oct. 16
Wilder, Thornton   April 17
Williams, Tennessee   Mar. 26
Williams, William Carlos   Sept. 17
Wilson, Angus   Aug. 11
Wilson, Edmund   May 8
Wolfe, Thomas   Oct. 3
Wolfe, Tom   Mar. 2
Woolf, Leonard   Nov. 25

Woolf, Virginia   Jan. 25
Woolson, Constance Fenimore   Mar. 5
Wordsworth, William   April 7
Wouk, Herman   May 27
Wright, Richard   Sept. 4
Wylie, Philip   May 12
Wyss, Johann   Mar. 4

Yeats, W. B.   June 13
Yerby, Frank   Sept. 5
Yevtushenko, Yevgeny   July 18
Yourcenar, Marguerite   June 8

Zangwill, Israel   Feb. 14
Zola, Emile   April 2

JOSEPH CONRAD • RUDYARD KIPLING • JANE AUSTEN • JONATHA

POUND • VOLTAIRE • E. M. FORSTER • J. D. SALINGER • ISA

DOCTOROW • GERALD DURRELL • SIMONE DE BEAUVOIR • JOHI

MILNE • LORD BYRON • EDITH WHARTON • ROBERT BURNS •

COLETTE • ANTON CHEKHOV • BARBARA TUCHMAN • JOHI

JAMES MICHENER • CHRISTOPHER MARLOWE • CHARLES LAMB

GEORGES SIMENON • TONI MORRISON • CARSON McCULLERS • W.

VICTOR HUGO • JOHN STEINBECK • HENRY WADSWORTI

BROWNING • GABRIEL GARCIA MARQUEZ • GEORGE ELIOT • VI

WILLIAM BLAKE • FLANNERY O'CONNOR • ROBERT FROST

ZOLA • WILLIAM WORDSWORTH • CHARLES BAUDELAIRE • SAMUE

• WILLIAM SHAKESPEARE • ANTHONY TROLLOPE • JOSEPI

ROBERT BROWNING • DANTE ALIGHIERI • HONORE DE BALZAC

CHESTERTON • WALT WHITMAN • MARGARET DRABBLE • SAUI

SARTRE • GEORGE ORWELL • JEAN JACQUES ROUSSEAU • TC

WILLIAM MAKEPEACE THACKERAY • ERNEST HEMINGWAY

GERARD MANLEY HOPKINS • LEON URIS • JOHN GALSWORTHY

WELLS • T. S. ELIOT • F. SCOTT FITZGERALD • WILLIAM FAULK

WILDE • GRAHAM GREENE • JOHN LE CARRÉ • DORIS LESSING